The Murder of Gabby Petito

The Tragic True Crime Story

Hunter Blackwell

To the memory of Gabrielle Petito, a vibrant young woman whose life was tragically cut short. This book is a testament to her spirit, a somber acknowledgment of the violence she endured, and a plea for a future where such tragedies are prevented. It is dedicated to her family and friends, who bravely navigated unimaginable grief while advocating for change and offering unwavering support to others grappling with similar pain. Their strength in the face of such profound loss serves as an inspiration to us all.

This work is also dedicated to the countless victims of domestic violence whose stories remain untold, whose suffering continues unseen. May this narrative serve as a reminder that their voices deserve to be heard, that their experiences deserve recognition, and that their lives deserve protection. We must strive to create a world where every individual, regardless of gender, background, or circumstance, feels safe, valued, and empowered. Furthermore, this book is dedicated to the individuals who dedicate their lives to combating domestic violence—the advocates, the counselors, the law enforcement officers, the social workers, and the countless others who work tirelessly to support survivors and bring abusers to justice. Your relentless commitment and unwavering compassion offer a beacon of hope in the darkness, a testament to the enduring power of human empathy and determination. The fight against domestic violence is a collective endeavor, and your contributions are invaluable.

Finally, this dedication extends to all those touched by the story of Gabby Petito and Brian Laundrie—the readers, the investigators, the journalists, the community members—who sought to understand, to learn, and to contribute to a better understanding of this complex and heartbreaking case. The outpouring of support and engagement with this tragedy showcases the power of collective empathy and the potential for positive change. May this book inspire reflection, ignite conversations, and ultimately contribute to a future free from the insidious grip of domestic violence.

Contents

Chapter One

The Wyoming Wilderness and the Discovery

The Setting Grand Teton National Park

The air hung crisp and cold, a stark contrast to the warmth of the sun beating down on the snow-capped peaks of the Teton Range. The vast expanse of Grand Teton National Park, usually a haven of breathtaking beauty, held a different, more somber energy in the autumn of 2021. The landscape, normally celebrated for its vibrant hues and teeming wildlife, was now draped in a cloak of quietude, a poignant backdrop to a tragedy that would forever stain its pristine wilderness.

The specific area where Gabby Petito's remains were found—a remote section of the Bridger-Teton National Forest, bordering the park—is a place of stark contrasts. Towering pines, their needles the color of aged bronze, clawed at the sky, their shadows stretching long and skeletal across the uneven terrain. The ground, a patchwork of muted greens and browns, was littered with fallen leaves, their vibrant colors muted by the encroaching winter. A glacial river, its icy waters carving a path through the landscape, flowed relentlessly onward, its constant murmur a lonely soundtrack to the stillness.

The beauty of the location was undeniable, even in its autumnal melancholy. The jagged peaks of the Tetons, piercing the pale blue sky, were a breathtaking sight, their majestic presence a testament to the power and enduring beauty of nature. Yet, this raw, untamed beauty was juxtaposed with the stark reality of the violence that had occurred within its embrace. The serene landscape was now irrevocably marked by the shadow of tragedy, a haunting reminder of the fragility of human life.

Imagine the scene: the crisp, mountain air biting at exposed skin; the silence punctuated only by the rustling of leaves and the distant call of a hawk. The sun, though high in the sky, cast long, eerie shadows that seemed to stretch and twist, mirroring the tangled emotions that gripped the investigators and the nation as the search for Gabby intensified. The sense of isolation was palpable, a chilling reminder of the vulnerability that Gabby had experienced in her final moments.

The sheer scale of the park itself contributed to the sense of isolation. Grand Teton National Park encompasses nearly 310,000 acres, a vast and unforgiving wilderness. Miles of winding trails, deep canyons, and dense forests offered countless places to hide, adding to the challenge of the search. The remote location where Gabby's body was found is accessible only by rugged, four-wheel-drive roads, making it even more difficult for rescuers to reach the site.

The landscape was not just a passive backdrop; it played an active role in the unfolding tragedy. The rugged terrain, the dense forests, the unpredictable weather – these were all factors that complicated the search and amplified the sense of urgency and dread. The very beauty of the place, in its untamed wildness, served as a cruel irony, a stark contrast to the violent end that Gabby met within its embrace.

The contrast between the vibrant, idealized image of Gabby's van life, meticulously documented on social media, and the stark reality of her death in this remote, unforgiving wilderness is striking. Her online presence painted a picture of carefree adventure, filled with stunning scenery and joyful experiences. The reality, however, was far more complex and tragically darker. The idyllic images stand in stark opposition to the harshness of the natural world and the violence that claimed her life.

The landscape itself seems to reflect this duality. The majestic peaks of the Tetons, symbolizing strength and permanence, are mirrored by the fragile vulnerability of human life. The flowing river, constantly moving forward, represents the relentless passage of time, the unstoppable march toward the inevitable. The silence of the wilderness, broken only by the wind and the distant cry of a bird, emphasizes the isolation and loneliness that accompanied Gabby in her final moments, a stark contrast to the often busy and connected world portrayed in her online presence.

The stark beauty of the Tetons is a powerful reminder of the enduring power of nature, a force both awe-inspiring and terrifying. It is a landscape that evokes a sense of both profound peace and profound solitude, a fitting reflection of the complex emotions that swirl around the tragedy of Gabby Petito's disappearance and death. The mountains stand tall, indifferent to human suffering, yet their silent majesty serves as a constant reminder of the precariousness of human existence against the backdrop of the vast, enduring wilderness.

The silence of the forest, broken only by the occasional snap of a twig or the rustle of leaves, is a powerful metaphor for the unanswered questions surrounding Gabby's death. The search for answers, like the search for her body in the vast expanse of the wilderness, was a painstaking and arduous process, each clue a piece of a puzzle slowly and painstakingly assembled. The vastness of the landscape mirrors the vastness of the grief felt by her family and friends, and the collective national mourning that followed the discovery of her body.

The details of the physical location – the specific trail, the type of vegetation, the proximity to water – all contribute to the evocative power of the setting. These details, meticulously recorded in police reports and forensic analyses, bring the landscape to life, transforming it from a distant, idealized image into a tangible, emotionally charged space, directly linked to the tragedy that unfolded.

Consider the subtle shifts in light, the way the sun dappled through the pines, casting long shadows that seemed to dance and writhe, a visual manifestation of the uncertainty and anxiety that surrounded the investigation. The cold, clear air, invigorating in its purity, yet simultaneously chilling in its starkness, reflects the emotional chill that settled over the nation as the details of Gabby's final days slowly emerged.

The contrast between the vibrant, colorful images captured in Gabby's social media posts – the bright blues of the sky, the greens of the foliage, the warm tones of her skin and clothing – and the somber, muted tones of the autumnal landscape where her body was found highlights the jarring juxtaposition between the idealized vision of her life and the harsh reality of her death. This visual contrast serves as a constant reminder of the deceptive nature of appearances and the fragility of life.

The details of the physical discovery—the location, the condition of the remains, the surrounding evidence—while grim, are crucial elements in understanding the narrative. These details, carefully pieced together by law enforcement and forensic experts, form the foundation of the investigation and contribute to the powerful narrative of the tragedy.

The careful recounting of these details helps to convey the raw emotion and the profound sense of loss that accompanied the discovery.

The Wyoming wilderness, in its stark beauty and unforgiving nature, served not only as the location of Gabby's final resting place, but also as a potent symbol of the larger narrative: a story of a young woman's life tragically cut short, a story of a failed relationship, a story of societal failings, and a story that ignited a national conversation about domestic violence and the complexities of human relationships in the digital age. The setting itself plays a crucial role in conveying the emotional weight of the tragedy. The stark beauty and inherent isolation of the landscape serve as a powerful counterpoint to the vibrant, idealized image of Gabby's van life, creating a poignant and unforgettable backdrop to this tragic story.

The Discovery Initial Police Response

The discovery was made on September 19th, 2021. The tip, received by law enforcement, was vague, a whisper in the vastness of the Bridger-Teton National Forest. It spoke of a possible body, located near a dispersed campsite, somewhere within the sprawling expanse of land encompassing millions of acres. The initial response was swift, even amidst the logistical challenges. The remoteness of the area, accessible only by rugged, four-wheel-drive trails, presented a significant hurdle. Helicopters, initially considered, were deemed unsuitable due to the dense forest canopy and uneven terrain. Instead, all-terrain vehicles and highly trained search and rescue teams were mobilized, their progress hampered by the uneven, rocky terrain and the thick undergrowth. The autumn air, crisp and cold, carried with it a sense of foreboding, as if the very wilderness itself was holding its breath.

The teams, comprised of park rangers, local law enforcement, and FBI agents, moved methodically, their movements guided by the sparse information provided in the tip. They were seasoned professionals, accustomed to the harsh realities of the wilderness, yet even their experience couldn't fully prepare them for what they were about to find. Days earlier, their search had been a frantic race against time, fueled by the ever-growing national concern and the relentless pressure from Gabby's anguished family. Now, the discovery promised an abrupt end to their exhaustive efforts, although the nature of that end was profoundly agonizing.

The moment of discovery was described in official reports as unemotional, stark, and clinical. Yet, those involved would never forget it. The details, released later in heavily redacted reports, paint a grim picture: a body, partially concealed by vegetation, near a shallow riverbed. The initial assessment suggested it was indeed Gabby Petito. The harsh realities of decomposition in the mountain wilderness had already begun their relentless work. The surrounding area yielded a trove of physical evidence – items that were carefully documented and cataloged for later analysis. Each piece, no matter how small or seemingly insignificant, held the potential to unlock crucial information about Gabby's last moments.

The discovery triggered a chain reaction. The quiet solitude of the Bridger-Teton was shattered by the arrival of more law enforcement personnel. The methodical precision of the initial search gave way to the intense activity of a full-scale crime scene investigation. The pristine wilderness, so recently a sanctuary of natural beauty, now became a stage for a tragedy unfolding in harsh relief. The investigators, weary but resolute, worked with a grim determination to ensure that every detail was captured, every clue preserved. Their work was hampered not only by the remote location, but also by the rapidly approaching winter. The threat of snow and freezing temperatures added urgency to their task, compelling them to work faster, more efficiently, even under the heavy weight of the somber occasion.

The initial steps taken were crucial. The area was secured, a perimeter established to protect the integrity of the crime scene. Forensic specialists, experts in their field, began their meticulous work, delicately collecting evidence, preserving its integrity for later laboratory analysis. Photographs were taken, videos were recorded, and every minute detail was documented with painstaking care. This detailed documentation served not only as evidence for the investigation, but also as a visual record of the scene, a solemn testament to the events that transpired. Later, this meticulous documentation would be subject to rigorous scrutiny, every detail meticulously examined, every decision justified, in the inevitable legal proceedings.

The challenge of transporting Gabby's remains out of the remote location was significant. The rugged terrain demanded the use of specialized equipment, adding hours to the already arduous process. Each step, each carefully planned movement, seemed laden with gravity, as if the weight of the world rested on the shoulders of the men and women involved. The raw emotion felt by the team was palpable. Though experienced in dealing with death, this case carried with it a uniquely poignant and tragic weight. The circumstances surrounding Gabby's disappearance had captured the nation's attention, her image plastered across news outlets, turning her into a symbol of the dangers facing young women and the systemic issues within law enforcement's approach to domestic violence cases. The quiet solemnity of their work was a stark contrast to the media frenzy surrounding the case.

The initial police reports, released in the days following the discovery, were guardedly worded, reflecting the sensitivity of the situation and the ongoing investigation. However, they acknowledged the identification of the body and confirmed the launch of a full-scale homicide investigation. The news, when finally made public, sent a ripple of grief and outrage across the country. The image of Gabby, bright and full of life in her social media posts, contrasted sharply with the reality of her tragic death. The details released, carefully chosen and measured, still sparked outrage and fueled public demand for answers, creating a wave of both grief and anger.

The ensuing investigation wouldn't just focus on the immediate circumstances of Gabby's death. It would delve deeper into the complexities of her relationship with Brian Laundrie, examine the social media narrative she crafted, and explore the systemic failures that may have contributed to the tragedy. The discovery in the Wyoming wilderness was not merely the finding of a body; it was the grim culmination of a much larger story, a story that would unfold over the coming weeks and months, a story that would captivate the nation and ignite a long-overdue national conversation about domestic violence and the power dynamics within intimate relationships.

The initial police response, in its logistical challenges and the profound emotional weight it carried, served as a microcosm of the wider narrative. It was a testament to the determination of law enforcement to bring justice to Gabby Petito, a young woman whose life was tragically cut short, a woman whose story continues to resonate with millions across the country and around the world.

The remoteness of the location, the harshness of the natural environment, and the weight of the tragedy served to highlight the extraordinary dedication of those involved, in their pursuit of justice and their solemn duty to honor her memory. The silence of the wilderness, the rustling of leaves, the cold mountain air – all formed a powerful backdrop to the initial efforts, underscoring both the challenge and the commitment of those involved in the investigation. The discovery in the Wyoming wilderness was the beginning, not the end, of a long and complex investigation.

The days following the discovery saw a flurry of activity. Teams continued to scour the surrounding area for additional evidence, meticulously collecting and preserving every piece of potential information. The terrain itself seemed to resist their efforts, presenting challenges at every turn. The investigation broadened, extending beyond the confines of the immediate crime scene to incorporate various other aspects. The investigation went beyond the physical evidence found at the site of the body. It incorporated information gathered from Gabby's digital footprint, her social media presence, her communications with friends and family, and the detailed reconstruction of her travels with Brian Laundrie. The investigators' work included interviews with individuals who had crossed paths with the couple during their road trip, piecing together the fragments of their journey to understand the dynamics of their relationship and the events that ultimately led to Gabby's death. The investigators moved from the stark silence of the Wyoming wilderness to the vibrant, yet deceptive, world of social media, where the curated images of a perfect road trip masked a reality far more sinister and dangerous.

The meticulous documentation of the crime scene, combined with the analysis of digital evidence and witness testimonies, would form the backbone of the investigation. Each piece of the puzzle, painstakingly collected and analyzed, was critical in reconstructing the events leading up to Gabby's death and ultimately bringing her killer to justice. The investigation into Gabby Petito's death underscored the need for a comprehensive approach to solving complex crimes, one that would involve collaboration among various agencies, technological prowess, and the dedication and perseverance of individuals from various backgrounds committed to achieving justice, even in the face of overwhelming challenges and extreme emotional toll. The initial police response in the Wyoming wilderness was simply the first, crucial step in a much longer journey towards understanding the tragedy and holding those responsible accountable.

The Calls Early Warnings

The discovery in the Wyoming wilderness marked a grim turning point, but the investigation had already been underway, albeit subtly, for weeks. The whispers of trouble, previously faint and easily dismissed, now echoed with the chilling clarity of hindsight. These whispers, initially lost in the din of daily life, had manifested in a series of 911 calls, each a fragmented snapshot of a deteriorating relationship, a chilling premonition of the tragedy to come. These calls, seemingly inconsequential at the time, would become crucial pieces of the puzzle, offering a disturbing glimpse into the escalating tension between Gabby and Brian Laundrie.

They would reveal not only the missed opportunities for intervention but also the inherent limitations of the 911 system in addressing the complexities of domestic violence. The first call, received by Moab City Police on August 12th, 2021, originated not from Gabby herself, but from a concerned witness. A frantic report detailed a domestic disturbance, a heated argument between a young couple near the Moonflower Community Cooperative. The caller, a bystander who had observed the altercation, described seeing Brian Laundrie forcefully shoving Gabby Petito into a van, before driving off. The description, while brief, painted a picture of escalating conflict, suggesting a level of aggression that warranted immediate attention.

The Moab police officers who responded to the scene arrived to find Gabby Petito visibly distraught, tears streaming down her face. Brian Laundrie, meanwhile, presented a far calmer demeanor, his words carefully chosen, his actions seemingly measured. The officers' body camera footage, later released to the public, captured the scene in stark detail. The contrast between Gabby's emotional distress and Brian's apparent composure underscored the inherent difficulties in assessing domestic disputes, particularly in situations where the victim's visible trauma might not fully align with their stated wishes.

The officers' initial assessment, as documented in their official report, determined that Gabby's emotional state might have been partly attributable to stress and anxiety related to the ongoing road trip. While they acknowledged the visible signs of emotional distress and the altercation reported by the witness, they ultimately chose to separate the couple for the night, and to advise them to seek counseling upon their return home. The decision, widely criticized in retrospect, highlighted a common challenge in domestic violence cases: the difficulty of establishing definitive proof of abuse when the victim's narrative may be inconsistent or hesitant, and the perpetrator presents a seemingly cooperative, if not entirely truthful, facade.

A second, crucial call, much more direct and distressing, came later, placing the events firmly within a pattern. This time, Gabby Petito herself was the caller. The call, abruptly ended before dispatch could fully assess the situation, revealed the deep anxiety in Gabby's voice. Her fragmented sentences, laced with pleas for help, indicated that a serious incident had occurred, though the precise details remained obscured by the brevity of the conversation and the muffled sounds in the background.

In the 911 audio, a portion of which was released to the public, the dispatch operator could be heard attempting to clarify Gabby's situation, only to be met with a series of confused responses and cries. The background noise suggested a struggle, a cacophony of shouts and the unmistakable sound of someone crying But the call terminated before Gabby could convey a clear location, an exact description of the incident, or an explicit statement about the level of immediate danger. The limitations of the brief and incomplete call serve as a stark reminder of the systemic challenges in handling domestic violence cases. Many times, victims, under immense stress and duress, may fail to convey the full extent of the danger they are facing.

The analysis of the 911 calls, particularly when viewed in conjunction with other evidence such as bodycam footage and witness testimonies, reveals a pattern of escalating tension and control. The initially subtle signs of conflict – the argument observed by the witness in Moab, the abrupt and emotionally charged call from Gabby herself – when considered together painted a much more disturbing picture than any individual incident might have suggested. Each call became an important data point, adding to a mosaic that ultimately revealed the dark reality of Gabby and Brian's relationship.

The release of these calls to the public sparked a wave of public outcry and intense media scrutiny. Critiques focused not only on the specific decisions made by law enforcement in Moab, but also on the broader challenges faced by agencies in addressing domestic violence, the difficulties of responding effectively to incomplete or ambiguous calls, and the overall limitations of the 911 system as a tool for preventing domestic abuse. The 911 calls, stripped of the context of a full investigation, provided only a limited perspective, yet they served as powerful symbolic representations of the complexities surrounding the case.

The conversations and their interpretations would fuel ongoing debates about law enforcement training, response protocols for domestic violence situations, and the need for improved methods of communicating with victims in distress. The calls also highlighted the urgent need for increased awareness among the public about the early warning signs of domestic abuse, the necessity of empowering victims to seek help, and the crucial importance of reporting even ambiguous situations of potential violence. The fragmented narratives within those calls, the incomplete sentences, the choked sobs, the background noise of chaos – all contributed to a larger narrative of missed opportunities, systemic failures, and a tragedy that could have potentially been averted. The 911 calls, therefore, extended far beyond being mere pieces of evidence; they transformed into poignant symbols of a flawed system grappling with the intricacies of domestic violence. The failures exposed were not merely failures of individual officers; they were systemic shortcomings, highlighting the need for comprehensive reforms within law enforcement and a broader societal shift in understanding and responding to domestic abuse.

The investigation expanded beyond the immediate responses to these calls, delving into the couple's digital footprint, their social media interactions, their communication with family and friends, and a careful reconstruction of their travels. The 911 calls served as a vital starting point, providing a framework for understanding the escalating tensions, the missed opportunities for intervention, and the overall context of a relationship that tragically ended in a remote corner of the Wyoming wilderness. The chilling silence of the calls, juxtaposed with the overwhelming public reaction following the discovery of Gabby Petito's body, underscored the profound impact of this tragedy and the urgent need for meaningful change. The incomplete narratives embedded within the 911 calls served as a tragic reminder of the complex nature of domestic violence and the inherent challenges faced by law enforcement in effectively responding to such incidents. The silence after the calls ended, the unresolved cries for help, stood as a stark testament to the need for more effective intervention strategies, improved training, and increased public awareness about the dangers of domestic abuse. The lingering questions surrounding the calls, the missed opportunities, the lack of decisive action, would continue to fuel discussions and debates long after the legal proceedings concluded. The analysis of these calls, therefore, became a crucial element in the larger investigation, shedding light on the systematic challenges and highlighting the urgent need for improved responses to domestic violence calls. The transcripts, the audio recordings, and the subsequent analysis would forever serve as a somber reminder of the human cost of systemic shortcomings and the importance of continuous improvement in the handling of domestic violence cases.

Social Media The Perfect Facade

The meticulously crafted Instagram feed, brimming with sun-drenched photographs of breathtaking landscapes and beaming smiles, offered a stark contrast to the chilling reality that unfolded in the Wyoming wilderness. Gabby Petito's online persona, a vibrant tapestry woven from picturesque sunsets, adventurous hikes, and affectionate snapshots with Brian Laundrie, presented a picture-perfect narrative of a carefree road trip. Each post, carefully curated and strategically captioned, projected an image of idyllic bliss, a seemingly unshakeable happiness that belied the underlying turmoil simmering beneath the surface.

Scrolling through Gabby's feed was like stepping into a meticulously designed travel brochure, each image a carefully selected moment, each caption a perfectly crafted sentence designed to evoke a sense of wonder and adventure. The van life aesthetic, so prevalent on social media, was flawlessly executed. There were shots of the couple embracing amidst towering redwoods, shots of them laughing over campfire meals under a star-studded sky, shots of breathtaking vistas that showcased their adventurous spirit. The carefully chosen filters enhanced the already captivating scenery, transforming each photo into a postcard-perfect memory. These images, shared with her followers, painted a picture of a young couple living their dream, traversing the country in a converted van, documenting their journey with breathtaking visuals and heartfelt captions.

However, beneath this carefully constructed façade, subtle inconsistencies and dissonances began to emerge upon closer examination. The frequency of the posts, initially consistent and regular, seemed to dwindle as their journey progressed. The captions, once brimming with enthusiasm and excitement, appeared shorter, less frequent, and lacking the infectious energy of the earlier posts. While the photos continued to portray a couple deeply in love, a keen observer might notice a subtle shift in Gabby's expressions. In some pictures, a hint of weariness, a fleeting shadow of sadness, could be detected in her eyes, a subtle dissonance that hinted at a reality that differed significantly from the carefully curated narrative.

The performative nature of social media relationships came into sharp focus. The curated images, the perfectly timed captions, the flawless aesthetics – all pointed to a conscious effort to present a specific image to the world, an idealized version of their reality. This performative aspect, so prevalent in the digital age, obscured the complexities of their relationship, making it difficult to discern the truth from the carefully constructed illusion. It highlighted the limitations of social media as a reliable source of information, particularly when it came to understanding the intricacies of human relationships. What was presented to the world was not necessarily an accurate reflection of the reality experienced behind closed doors.

Brian Laundrie's online presence, though less prolific than Gabby's, further complicated the narrative. His posts, fewer and less frequent than Gabby's, added another layer to the carefully constructed online persona. The relative scarcity of his contributions to their shared online chronicle raised questions about his level of participation in the narrative and the extent to which he was involved in crafting the idyllic image they projected to the outside world. The contrast between Gabby's frequent and enthusiastic posts and Brian's infrequent and more reserved updates suggested a power imbalance, a subtle disparity in their control over their shared narrative.

The careful study of their social media interactions revealed a pattern of subtle shifts and inconsistencies. The playful banter, the heartfelt comments, and the public declarations of affection, prevalent in the early stages of their journey, appeared to diminish as time went on. While some posts still maintained a semblance of normalcy, the overall tone and frequency suggested a gradual erosion of their shared joy and a growing distance between them. This subtle shift, easily missed by casual observers, became a critical piece of the puzzle when viewed in the context of the subsequent investigation.

Examining their comments sections revealed a further layer of complexity. While many followers showered the couple with praise and encouragement, a few astute commentators noticed the subtle shift in tone and expressed concern over Gabby's apparent unhappiness in some of the later photos. These observations, though largely ignored at the time, serve as a chilling testament to the power of collective observation and the potential for social media to reveal underlying truths, even when obscured by a carefully curated facade. The comments, initially disregarded as mere fleeting observations, became valuable pieces of the puzzle during the subsequent investigation, reinforcing the idea that even the smallest details can provide crucial insights into a complex situation.

Experts in digital forensics, brought in to analyze their social media activity, meticulously scrutinized their posts, comments, and interactions, looking for subtle clues that might shed light on the deteriorating nature of their relationship. Their analysis extended beyond simply examining the content of their posts to encompass the metadata associated with the images, including geolocation data and timestamps. This analysis provided crucial clues that helped investigators piece together a timeline of their movements and activities, further reinforcing the narrative emerging from other sources of evidence.

The digital footprint of Gabby and Brian Laundrie offered a unique insight into the complexities of their relationship, providing a glimpse into the carefully constructed narrative they presented to the world and the subtle cracks that revealed the underlying truth. The contrast between the idyllic images they shared online and the grim reality of their demise highlighted the inherent limitations of social media as a reliable source of information and underscored the importance of critical thinking and careful analysis in navigating the complexities of the digital world. The meticulous analysis of their social media presence became a crucial element in the broader investigation, adding a layer of depth and complexity to the unfolding narrative. Their online world, once a seemingly idyllic representation of their lives, became a valuable source of evidence, revealing subtle hints of the underlying tension and ultimately providing valuable context to the events that led to the tragic end of their journey. The digital breadcrumbs they left behind, initially dismissed as inconsequential details of a happy couple's road trip, became crucial pieces of the puzzle, ultimately helping to unravel the layers of deception and reveal the dark secrets concealed beneath the carefully constructed facade of their online personas.

The National Attention A Media Frenzy

The discovery of Gabby Petito's body in the vast expanse of Grand Teton National Park ignited a firestorm of media attention, transforming a missing person's case into a national obsession almost overnight. The 24-hour news cycle, fueled by the relentless appetite for breaking news and the immediacy of social media, seized upon the story with a ferocity that overwhelmed the investigation itself. Cable news networks dedicated hours of coverage to the case, replaying the same snippets of video, analyzing the same social media posts, and speculating endlessly on the whereabouts of Brian Laundrie. Websites and blogs dedicated to true crime exploded with commentary, theories, and amateur sleuthing, transforming the internet into a virtual town square buzzing with conjecture and speculation.

The sheer volume of media coverage was unprecedented. Every detail, no matter how seemingly insignificant, was dissected, analyzed, and endlessly debated. The couple's social media posts, initially viewed as charming glimpses into their van life adventure, were now scrutinized for hidden clues and potential foreshadowing. Each photograph, each caption, each comment became a piece of evidence in the ongoing media trial, subjected to intense scrutiny and interpretation. The public, captivated by the story's tragic unfolding, devoured every morsel of information, transforming Gabby and Brian into household names.

The intense media scrutiny had a profound impact on the investigation. Law enforcement agencies, already grappling with the complexities of a cross-state investigation, found themselves under immense public pressure to deliver results. The constant barrage of news reports, social media commentary, and speculation created an environment of heightened anxiety and pressure, potentially compromising the integrity of the investigation. The constant updates and speculative reporting created a challenging environment for law enforcement, forcing them to balance the need to provide timely information to the public with the imperative to maintain the integrity of their investigation. The intense media spotlight hampered the investigative process, potentially contaminating evidence and influencing witness statements.

Social media platforms, originally intended as a means of connection and sharing, became a battleground for competing narratives. The constant flow of information, much of it unsubstantiated and often misleading, created confusion and fueled speculation. The rapid spread of misinformation and the proliferation of conspiracy theories further complicated the investigation, diverting attention from the facts and fueling public distrust. Many well-meaning individuals, eager to contribute to the search effort, inadvertently hindered the investigation by spreading rumors and misinformation. The digital landscape became a breeding ground for speculation and misinformation, highlighting the challenges of managing information in the age of social media.

The role of social media in amplifying the story was undeniable. Gabby's Instagram account, once a showcase of their idyllic road trip, became a focal point of the media frenzy. The contrast between her carefully curated online persona and the grim reality of her demise created a captivating narrative that resonated with millions. The public's fascination with the case was amplified by the constant flow of information, speculation, and amateur detective work taking place online. Millions followed the case online, sharing theories, speculating on Brian's whereabouts, and offering condolences to Gabby's family.

The 24-hour news cycle exacerbated the situation. The need for constant updates and fresh content led to a relentless pursuit of information, often at the expense of accuracy and sensitivity. News outlets competed for viewers and clicks, leading to a sometimes sensationalized and overly dramatic portrayal of events. The constant pressure to provide breaking news and insightful analysis often blurred the lines between reporting and speculation. In the rush to provide immediate updates, the nuances and complexities of the case were often overlooked or oversimplified.

The ethical implications of reporting on such a sensitive case were significant. The media's responsibility was not merely to report the facts but also to protect the integrity of the investigation and to avoid causing further harm to the victims' families. The constant media attention undoubtedly increased the emotional distress experienced by Gabby's family, forcing them to relive the tragedy through countless news reports and social media posts. The ethical considerations of reporting on a sensitive case involving a missing person and subsequent homicide required a careful balance between informing the public and respecting the privacy of those involved.

However, the media's role was not entirely negative. The intense public interest generated by the coverage, while problematic in some aspects, also put immense pressure on law enforcement to expedite the investigation. The constant public scrutiny served as a deterrent against any attempts to obstruct justice or cover up crucial details. The media's intense focus on the case undoubtedly contributed to the swiftness of the investigation and the arrest of Brian Laundrie, albeit after a period of intensive public speculation.

The Gabby Petito case became a stark reminder of the complexities and challenges of covering true crime in the digital age. The intensity of media coverage, fueled by social media and the 24-hour news cycle, highlighted the need for responsible journalism, ethical considerations, and a balanced approach to reporting on sensitive and high-profile cases. The delicate balance between informing the public and protecting the integrity of the investigation became a central theme in the media's coverage of the case.

The media frenzy surrounding the case also served as a catalyst for broader conversations about domestic violence, missing persons, and the challenges faced by law enforcement in the digital age. The intense public interest in the case led to increased awareness of the prevalence of domestic violence and the need for improved support systems for victims. The tragedy of Gabby's death spurred policy changes and reforms aimed at enhancing the response to missing persons cases.

In the aftermath of the media frenzy, discussions arose concerning media ethics, particularly regarding the need for responsible reporting in sensitive cases. The debate centered on the balance between informing the public and potentially jeopardizing the investigation, as well as the emotional well-being of those involved.

The impact of the relentless media scrutiny on the families of both Gabby Petito and Brian Laundrie brought to the forefront the importance of ethical considerations in covering sensitive true crime stories. The case served as a case study in responsible media practices, particularly in relation to the coverage of true crime events in the digital age.

The case highlighted the transformative power of social media in shaping public perception and influencing investigations. While social media proved to be a double-edged sword, facilitating the rapid dissemination of information while also amplifying misinformation and speculation, its impact on the Gabby Petito case was undeniable. The events surrounding the case underscored the critical need for responsible reporting, ethical considerations, and the judicious use of social media in the coverage of high-profile true crime events. The legacy of the case serves as a valuable lesson for both law enforcement and the media in navigating the complex intersection of investigations, social media, and the need for responsible reporting. The intense media scrutiny and subsequent public outcry surrounding the Gabby Petito case underscored the need for a responsible approach to covering high-profile true crime events, emphasizing the delicate balance between keeping the public informed and maintaining the integrity of the investigation. The case also prompted wider discussions about the impact of social media on criminal investigations and the importance of media ethics in reporting on sensitive cases.

Chapter Two

The Road Trip

A Descent into Chaos

The Van Life Idealized and Real

The idyllic image of van life, meticulously crafted and curated for Instagram feeds, presents a stark contrast to the harsh realities faced by Gabby and Brian. The romanticized vision—sun-drenched landscapes, spontaneous adventures, and unwavering freedom—obscured the inherent challenges of prolonged close-quarters living and the immense pressure placed on a relationship already teetering on the brink. Their journey, initially conceived as an escape, quickly transformed into a pressure cooker, amplifying existing tensions and exposing vulnerabilities that ultimately proved fatal.

The van, intended as their sanctuary and mobile home, became a confining space, a microcosm of their deteriorating relationship. The constant proximity, the lack of personal space, and the ever-present awareness of each other's moods created an environment ripe for conflict. What began as a shared adventure evolved into a claustrophobic existence, stripping away the veneer of their carefully constructed online persona and revealing the raw, unfiltered friction of their daily lives. Simple inconveniences—a leaky faucet, a malfunctioning appliance, a disagreement over the route—were amplified in the confined space, escalating into arguments that chipped away at their already fragile bond.

The logistical challenges of van life further exacerbated their difficulties. Finding suitable campsites, managing limited resources, and dealing with unexpected breakdowns all added to their stress levels. The constant need to plan, to adapt, and to problem-solve placed a significant strain on their emotional reserves, pushing them to their limits. The idealized version of van life often overlooks the mundane realities—the constant need for maintenance, the challenges of finding reliable internet access, and the logistical hurdles of navigating unfamiliar territories. Gabby and Brian's experience reveals the stark difference between the carefully curated aesthetic of van life on social media and the often-grueling reality of life on the road.

The pressure to maintain a flawless online presence added another layer of complexity to their journey. The need to portray a picture of effortless adventure and unwavering happiness meant concealing the underlying cracks in their relationship. Their meticulously crafted Instagram posts, designed to project an image of idyllic bliss, concealed the growing resentment and friction beneath the surface. The constant need to curate their online persona created a pressure cooker of internal conflict, forcing them to present a version of themselves that was far from the reality. This inherent dishonesty, this attempt to maintain a facade, only served to deepen the fissures in their relationship, creating an unsustainable emotional burden.

Beyond the logistical and external pressures, the isolated nature of their journey had a significant impact on their mental health. The constant togetherness, the lack of external support networks, and the absence of regular social interaction created an environment of intense intimacy and isolation. This lack of external perspective, this absence of a neutral sounding board, amplified their individual vulnerabilities and fueled the negativity between them. The lack of social interaction with other people contributed to the isolation, and the isolation, in turn, created an atmosphere of constant tension and mistrust. Their mental states were further compounded by the challenges of living in close quarters, managing limited resources, and enduring the stresses of daily life on the road. Their internal struggles amplified within the confined space of their van and further alienated each other.

The van life, far from the escapist fantasy they had envisioned, became a crucible for their internal conflicts. The lack of space to escape each other meant that their tensions were always present, always simmering beneath the surface. The constant proximity exacerbated the underlying tensions, fueling arguments and creating an atmosphere of constant friction. This constant tension contributed to an atmosphere of distrust and uncertainty, making it difficult for them to communicate and resolve their issues effectively. They were trapped not only in their van, but also in a cycle of arguments, accusations, and escalating conflict. The dream of freedom and escape transformed into a prison of their own making.

The pressure of their relationship was further compounded by the expectations of their online audience. The constant need to maintain a positive image of their adventure, the pressure to present a picture of perfection to their followers, added another layer of strain. Each post, each photograph, each caption became another act of performance, another attempt to maintain a façade that was crumbling from within. This constant pressure to portray an idealized version of themselves created an added stress that was impossible to sustain in the long run. The facade of their online relationship crumbled under the weight of their real-life struggles.

One could argue that the confinement of their van mirrored the confinement of their relationship. The intimate, small space magnified their conflicts and prevented any opportunity for needed distance or perspective. This constant togetherness, intended as an escape, morphed into a catalyst for their relationship's unraveling, with nowhere to escape the cycle of arguments and misunderstandings. Each day, the problems piled up, the pressures intensified, and the once-promising adventure transformed into a relentless struggle for survival, both for the relationship and their individual well-being.

The psychological toll of their van life adventure is evident in their interactions captured on video and through recovered social media posts. The increasing tension and irritability present a stark contrast to the initial enthusiasm and joy captured earlier in their journey. A gradual shift in demeanor, a perceptible change in their communication styles, points to the immense pressure they were enduring. The careful curation of their social media profiles hides the darker reality of their mental health challenges and the mounting strain on their relationship.

In conclusion, the romanticized notion of van life serves as a poignant backdrop to the tragic story of Gabby and Brian. Their experience serves as a cautionary tale, highlighting the deceptive allure of an idealized lifestyle and the potential for disastrous consequences when reality clashes with expectations. The constraints of their chosen lifestyle, coupled with the stresses of their relationship, ultimately led to a tragic outcome, underscoring the importance of recognizing and addressing the challenges of close-quarters living and the potential psychological impact of an isolated and pressure-filled existence. Their story stands as a reminder of the hidden dangers lurking beneath the seemingly idyllic surface of social media perfection.

Conflict and Confrontation A Timeline of Events

The initial weeks of their journey painted a picture of youthful exuberance on social media. Gabby's meticulously crafted Instagram posts showcased breathtaking landscapes and spontaneous adventures, a carefully curated narrative of freedom and bliss. Brian, often present in the background of these idyllic scenes, appeared to be a supportive partner, contributing to the illusion of a perfect couple embarking on a dream vacation. However, behind this polished facade, subtle cracks were beginning to appear, hinted at in the occasional cryptic caption or a slightly strained smile in a photograph. These were subtle indications, easily missed amidst the stunning scenery and carefully constructed narrative.

Analysis of their social media activity reveals a gradual shift in tone and content. Early posts radiated positivity and excitement, filled with details about their planned itinerary and spontaneous detours. As the weeks progressed, however, the posts became less frequent, and the tone shifted from joyful enthusiasm to a more subdued, almost melancholic tone. The vibrant colors and carefree poses gave way to more muted images, reflecting the changing dynamics of their relationship. The vibrant landscapes seem to mirror the decaying nature of their relationship.

While the public image projected an image of harmony, accounts from individuals who briefly encountered the couple paint a contrasting picture. A Moab, Utah, police report, detailing a domestic dispute, offers a stark counterpoint to the carefully crafted online persona. This incident, although initially dismissed as a minor disagreement, serves as a significant turning point, a clear indication that the carefully cultivated image of idyllic harmony was beginning to crumble. Witnesses described seeing an agitated Brian and a visibly distressed Gabby, their words hinting at a deeper underlying tension that extended beyond a simple argument.

The initial report described the couple as having engaged in a shouting match, leading to a short separation, but the underlying discord was clearly palpable. The incident highlights the potential volatility beneath the surface of their carefully curated social media presence. The report, a seemingly minor detail, provided critical evidence of escalating tension. The fact that Gabby had to be separated from Brian before she was calm enough to speak with officers was a clear indication that something deeper was wrong.

The incident in Moab marked a clear shift in the trajectory of their journey. What had started as a hopeful adventure, a chance to escape the pressures of everyday life and reconnect, quickly devolved into a tense and increasingly volatile environment. Subsequent social media posts, while still attempting to maintain a positive image, revealed subtle signs of strain. Gabby's captions became less detailed, her usual exuberance replaced by a quietness that hinted at underlying emotional distress. Brian's presence in the photographs seemed less enthusiastic, his smiles more forced, revealing the strain of the ongoing conflict.

The available video footage, including snippets captured on Gabby's phone, provides a chilling insight into their deteriorating relationship. The videos, while incomplete and often short, capture snippets of heated arguments, showcasing escalating tension and increasingly hostile interactions. The tone and body language of both individuals reveal a significant deterioration in their emotional connection. The videos, often interspersed with stunning visuals of the landscape, create a jarring contrast between the beauty of their surroundings and the ugliness of their conflict. One particular video segment, where Brian is seen aggressively pulling Gabby away from their van during an argument, stands out as particularly disturbing, hinting at a level of physical aggression that underscores the severity of their conflict. The small snippets of footage offer crucial insight into the reality of their relationship, painting a far more disturbing picture than their carefully curated social media posts. While these moments are brief and do not provide a complete narrative, they add invaluable context to the overall picture of their deteriorating relationship.

Further evidence emerged from text messages and phone calls between Gabby and her family. These communications, meticulously documented and analyzed, reveal a growing sense of anxiety and distress on Gabby's part. Her messages conveyed increasingly frequent concerns about Brian's behavior, describing instances of controlling behavior, escalating arguments, and her mounting fear for her safety. Although her messages were carefully worded, often attempting to downplay the severity of the situation, subtle clues—a change in her usual upbeat tone, an increased frequency of communication, and repeated requests for assistance—reveal the extent of her growing distress. These communications offer a crucial window into Gabby's innermost feelings and the severity of her circumstances.

As their road trip progressed, the frequency and intensity of their conflicts escalated. Witnesses at various campsites reported hearing loud arguments emanating from their van, further confirming the deteriorating state of their relationship. These accounts provide additional corroboration to the picture painted by the available digital evidence and Gabby's communications with family and friends. The testimonies describe arguments ranging from minor disagreements over trivial matters to more serious confrontations involving shouting and accusations, indicative of an escalating conflict that was steadily eroding the foundation of their relationship. The consistency of these accounts strongly suggests a pattern of escalating conflict, underscoring the deteriorating dynamic between Gabby and Brian.

The final days of Gabby's life are particularly shrouded in uncertainty, with limited verifiable information available. However, by piecing together the fragmented evidence—cell phone records, social media activity, and the accounts of those who had contact with the couple—it becomes evident that their relationship had reached a critical breaking point. This final phase is characterized by a notable lack of communication from Gabby and escalating concern from her family, setting the stage for the tragic events that followed. The lack of communication coupled with mounting concern from her family is a crucial aspect that contributed to the subsequent frantic search and the eventual tragic discovery.

This timeline of conflict and confrontation underscores the tragic escalation of events leading to Gabby's death. The carefully curated Instagram persona, the seemingly idyllic road trip, was a far cry from the reality of a relationship characterized by growing tension, escalating arguments, and a pervasive atmosphere of fear. The evidence clearly demonstrates a pattern of escalating conflict, highlighting the dangers of unhealthy relationships and the importance of recognizing the warning signs. While Gabby's online presence projected a picture of happiness and adventure, her real-life experiences reveal a different story, emphasizing the deceptive nature of social media and the importance of looking beneath the surface. The meticulous reconstruction of events serves as a stark reminder of the fragility of life and the devastating consequences of unchecked conflict within a relationship. The story of Gabby and Brian's road trip serves not only as a cautionary tale but also as a tribute to the victims of domestic violence and a call for increased awareness and preventative measures. The meticulously researched timeline serves as a powerful testament to the importance of recognizing and responding to the signs of domestic violence.

The Moab Incident A Missed Opportunity

The Moab incident, a seemingly minor domestic dispute initially dismissed by law enforcement, now stands as a chilling turning point in the narrative of Gabby and Brian's tragic journey. The details, painstakingly pieced together from police reports, body camera footage, and witness accounts, reveal a missed opportunity, a potential intervention that might have altered the course of events. The 911 call, initiated by a concerned bystander who witnessed an altercation between Gabby and Brian, sparked the initial police response. The caller described an agitated Brian and a visibly distraught Gabby, their interaction escalating into a shouting match near the entrance of a grocery store. The report details Brian's visibly agitated state, his hands shaking, as he explained the situation to the officers. Gabby, conversely, appeared visibly distressed, tears streaming down her face as she recounted the events leading up to the altercation.

The body camera footage, a crucial piece of evidence, captures the officers' initial interaction with the couple. The footage shows the officers engaging in separate interviews with Brian and Gabby, seeking to understand the nature of the conflict. Brian's account, while containing elements of truth, also displayed a calculated effort to minimize the gravity of the situation. His narrative painted a picture of a minor disagreement, a lovers' quarrel, easily resolved. However, inconsistencies in his story, and the officers' observations of his body language and tone, hinted at a deeper, more troubling dynamic. He often averted eye contact, his voice occasionally rising in pitch, betraying the composure he attempted to project. His physical demeanor, as noted in the police report and documented by the footage, seemed to contradict his relatively calm verbal account. The officers were unable to reconcile Brian's words with his visibly agitated demeanor.

Gabby's account is equally revealing, albeit heavily affected by the emotional distress she was visibly experiencing. Her fragmented narrative, interspersed with tears and hesitant pauses, paints a disturbing picture of control and manipulation. She described feeling overwhelmed and manipulated, and that this was not the first instance of such behavior. Her narrative hints at a pattern of controlling behavior by Brian, which was further confirmed by later recovered text messages and accounts from friends and family. Gabby's emotional state made it difficult for her to fully articulate the extent of her fears and concerns, further illustrating the difficulties faced by victims of domestic violence in communicating the full extent of the abuse. Despite her obvious emotional distress, and Brian's obvious agitation, the officers appeared to focus on the superficial aspects of the incident, seemingly dismissing the undercurrents of fear and control.

The officers, faced with a complex situation, attempted to de-escalate the tension by encouraging Brian and Gabby to separate for the night. The rationale behind this decision, as noted in the report, was based on their assessment of the situation as a "minor domestic dispute." However, the body camera footage reveals an apparent lack of thorough investigation into the underlying dynamics of the conflict. The officers did not delve deeply into Gabby's account of the situation. They failed to adequately address the signs of fear and distress that she exhibited, instead prioritizing a rapid resolution of the immediate conflict. Furthermore, the officers' interaction lacked any exploration of the history of the relationship and of the possibility of ongoing abusive behavior. The report lacked any reference to Gabby's fears concerning Brian's behavior, suggesting a lack of awareness or prioritization of those concerns. While the officers acted according to their training and experience at the time, the approach lacked the sensitivity and depth of investigation that a situation of potential domestic violence warrants.

The officers' approach is reflective of the wider challenges faced by law enforcement in dealing with domestic violence cases. The difficulties in identifying and responding appropriately to the complexities of abusive relationships are well-documented. The subtle cues, the undercurrents of fear and manipulation, are often masked by seemingly minor disagreements or surface-level conflict. The police encounter in Moab serves as a stark reminder of these challenges, highlighting the inherent difficulties of accurately assessing the gravity of domestic violence situations within a limited timeframe. The police response exemplifies the frequent difficulties faced by law enforcement in navigating the complexities of domestic violence cases, highlighting the subtle cues and the potential for misinterpretation.

Reviewing the police report and body camera footage, it's evident that the officers could have adopted a more proactive and comprehensive approach. A deeper investigation into Gabby's statements, a more in-depth questioning of Brian, and possibly a referral to domestic violence resources, could have averted the tragic events that unfolded later. The lack of a deeper investigation, coupled with the focus on immediate conflict resolution, ultimately resulted in a missed opportunity to identify and address the potential for future harm. The emphasis on immediate de-escalation of the current conflict seemingly overshadowed the potential for future escalation, a critical oversight in domestic violence situations. The Moab incident underscores the fact that a seemingly minor dispute can be a harbinger of more serious problems. The focus on the immediate conflict, while aiming for de-escalation, neglected the potential for future, far more serious, consequences.

The aftermath of the Moab incident revealed the limitations of the initial response, highlighting the need for more comprehensive training and awareness among law enforcement regarding domestic violence. The lack of a thorough investigation into Gabby's account of events, coupled with the apparent dismissal of her visible distress, stands as a significant point of criticism. The incident became the focus of subsequent investigations and reports, shedding light on the shortcomings in the initial response and emphasizing the need for improved protocols for dealing with domestic violence situations.

The Moab incident remains a critical element in the tragic narrative of Gabby and Brian's road trip, serving as a pivotal moment where a potential intervention was missed. The analysis of the police encounter, through the lens of police reports and body camera footage, highlights not only the complexities of domestic violence but also the potential consequences of inadequate responses. The incident underscores the need for continued improvements in law enforcement training, protocols, and awareness regarding domestic violence, a call for action in the hope that such tragic oversights can be prevented in the future. The scrutiny of this incident serves as a sobering reminder of the limitations of reactive law enforcement and the necessity for proactive measures in preventing domestic violence tragedies. The missed opportunity in Moab serves as a powerful case study in the challenges and complexities of addressing domestic violence, urging a renewed commitment to education and training within law enforcement agencies. The meticulous examination of this incident has brought into sharp relief the systemic challenges related to domestic violence intervention, suggesting that a comprehensive approach is necessary to address the problem fully. The case underscores the urgency for improved training and a more proactive approach to domestic violence, one that emphasizes thorough investigation and a deep understanding of the dynamics at play within such relationships.

The Last Days A Reconstruction

The investigation into Gabby Petito's disappearance, initially hampered by the vastness of the Wyoming wilderness and the complexities of a cross-country road trip, began to yield crucial details as investigators pieced together the final fragments of her life. The meticulous analysis of her social media activity, a seemingly innocuous collection of photographs and posts, offered a chilling counterpoint to the idyllic images she projected. While her Instagram feed portrayed a carefree adventure, a closer examination revealed subtle shifts in her demeanor, a gradual erosion of the cheerful persona she meticulously crafted for her online audience. The frequency of her posts decreased, the vibrant colors and enthusiastic captions replaced by a quietude that foreshadowed the tragedy to come.

A particularly poignant series of photos showcased the couple's visit to Grand Teton National Park. The images, seemingly innocuous snapshots of breathtaking scenery, upon closer inspection, reveal a subtle change in Gabby's posture. Her usual radiant smile, a constant feature in her previous posts, seems strained, almost forced. Her eyes, once bright and full of life, appear weary and shadowed, betraying a deeper sadness not apparent in the carefully curated images. The photographs, meticulously analyzed by investigators, revealed a subtle shift in her body language, a silent scream buried beneath a veneer of forced cheerfulness. The images became a visual testament to the escalating tension within the relationship. A forensic analysis of the metadata associated with the photographs—GPS coordinates, timestamps, and camera settings—provided crucial insights into Gabby's movements and the timeline of events.

The timeline, reconstructed from various sources, begins to coalesce around the last confirmed sighting of Gabby in Jackson Hole, Wyoming. Eyewitness accounts place her at a local restaurant, dining with Brian. While the encounter itself was unremarkable, the details provided by witnesses are significant. One witness described seeing Brian acting unusually agitated, his voice raised during a brief argument with Gabby. Though the incident seemed trivial at the time, it serves as another unsettling data point in the growing narrative of escalating tension. These seemingly insignificant details, often overlooked in the initial stages of the investigation, gain critical significance as the puzzle of Gabby's final days unfolds. The restaurant staff, initially reluctant to participate, eventually came forward after media coverage of the case. Their recollections, initially dismissed as inconsequential, would later become vital pieces of evidence in reconstructing the final moments.

Further information surfaced from a local gas station attendant who recalled seeing Gabby and Brian fill up their van on August 25th. The attendant's description of their interaction, albeit brief, painted a picture of subtle discord. While both seemed polite, a lingering sense of discomfort, a palpable tension, was noted. This was substantiated by another independent witness, a hiker who encountered the couple on a trail in Grand Teton. While acknowledging a cordial exchange, the hiker mentioned a palpable sense of unease surrounding Brian, an almost palpable sense of tension that couldn't be ignored. The hiker's account added another layer to the growing sense of unease surrounding Brian's behaviour during these last days.

The investigation also involved a close examination of Brian Laundrie's movements during this critical period. Cell phone records, meticulously obtained with appropriate warrants, revealed his movements in the days leading up to Gabby's disappearance. These records showed a significant shift in his activity, with frequent changes in location, hinting at attempts to conceal his whereabouts. The analysis of cell phone tower triangulation provided insights into the trajectory of his movements, helping law enforcement narrow down the possible areas of interest. Crucially, the data showed a significant overlap in his movements with the known location of Gabby's last known location. The seemingly mundane data points—cell tower pings, location-based timestamps—revealed a pattern of deliberate obfuscation, underlining the growing suspicion surrounding Brian's involvement in Gabby's disappearance.

Social media data continued to play a significant role in the investigation. Brian Laundrie's social media activity, or rather the conspicuous absence thereof, further fueled suspicion. While Gabby's social media presence abruptly ceased, Brian's silence, particularly his lack of posts or updates expressing concern about Gabby's disappearance, was deemed particularly unsettling. His last post, an innocuous image of a landscape, seemed almost tauntingly dismissive of the gravity of the situation. Digital forensic experts scrutinized his account for any hidden messages or deleted posts, any hint that might shed further light on his actions. While no such overt clues were discovered, the absence of any genuine expression of concern was striking, a stark contrast to the public outcry from Gabby's family and friends.

Further examination of Gabby's personal belongings, recovered from the van, revealed another crucial piece of the puzzle: a journal. The journal entries, penned in Gabby's own hand, provided intimate insights into her deteriorating mental state. The entries document the increasing strain on the relationship, detailing instances of Brian's controlling behavior and emotional manipulation. These intimate accounts offered a chilling perspective into the dark side of their adventure, a stark contrast to the meticulously crafted image presented on social media. The entries described growing feelings of fear and isolation, a sense of being trapped within a relationship that had become increasingly toxic. The journal became a critical piece of evidence, providing a powerful firsthand account of the emotional turmoil Gabby experienced in the final days of her life.

The police, building on all these strands of evidence, intensified their search efforts. Focusing on the areas highlighted by cell phone data and witness accounts, the investigation expanded to encompass a wider geographical area. Drone footage, advanced search techniques, and the involvement of specialized units all contributed to the search efforts, highlighting the collaborative nature of the investigation. The sheer scale of the operation, involving multiple agencies and specialized units, underscored the gravity of the situation and the determination of law enforcement to find Gabby and bring her to safety. The intense public scrutiny of the investigation was a catalyst, compelling law enforcement to act with speed and efficiency. The mounting pressure from the public, the media, and Gabby's family intensified the urgency of the search, ensuring that no stone was left unturned.

The final piece of the puzzle, the discovery of Gabby's body, brought the agonizing search to a tragic end. The location of the body, its proximity to areas identified by cell phone data and witness accounts, confirmed the accuracy of the timeline and corroborated the suspicions surrounding Brian's involvement. The subsequent autopsy confirmed the cause of death, providing a critical confirmation of the events that had unfolded. The discovery of the body marked a pivotal moment in the investigation, shifting the focus from a missing person case to a homicide investigation. The grim reality of the situation served as a stark reminder of the dangers of domestic violence and the devastating consequences of abuse. The finding highlighted the imperative need for improved strategies for identifying and intervening in abusive relationships, emphasizing the need for greater awareness and proactive intervention.

The meticulous reconstruction of Gabby Petito's last days, though harrowing, offers a poignant lesson in the interconnectedness of digital evidence, eyewitness testimony, and traditional investigative techniques. The integration of these diverse sources, the meticulous attention to detail, and the sheer collaborative effort involved served as a stark reminder of the complexities and challenges inherent in modern-day crime investigation. The story of Gabby Petito is a cautionary tale, a tragic illustration of the hidden dangers that can lurk within seemingly idyllic relationships, a story that underscores the ongoing need for greater awareness, education, and preventative measures in addressing the pervasive problem of domestic violence. The meticulous reconstruction also sheds light on the importance of technology, both in perpetuating the cycle of violence and in the eventual unraveling of the truth.

Brian Laundries Actions A Puzzle of Deception

The discovery of Gabby Petito's body shifted the investigative focus dramatically. No longer a missing person case, the investigation transformed into a full-scale homicide inquiry, with Brian Laundrie instantly becoming the prime suspect. The scrutiny intensified, the public's gaze fixated on his every move, or rather, his lack thereof. His silence was deafening, a stark contrast to the outpouring of grief and outrage surrounding Gabby's death. The pressure mounted, not just from law enforcement, but from the relentless media coverage and the unwavering demands for justice from Gabby's family and the public at large.

Laundrie's initial response to the burgeoning investigation was characterized by calculated silence. He returned home to North Port, Florida, without Gabby, driving her van, a vehicle that had become a central piece of the evidence puzzle. This act alone, a silent, yet profoundly significant gesture, hinted at a deeper level of culpability. His refusal to cooperate with law enforcement immediately raised alarm bells. Instead of offering assistance, he retreated, effectively creating a wall of silence that further fueled suspicion. The carefully crafted narrative he presented—a story of a distraught young man whose girlfriend had simply vanished—began to unravel under the weight of mounting evidence.

His parents' involvement, while initially presented as one of supportive concern, soon came under intense scrutiny. Their actions, initially seemingly innocuous, began to appear increasingly suspicious. Their refusal to directly assist investigators, their evasiveness during interrogations, and the inconsistencies in their accounts all contributed to the growing perception of a deliberate cover-up. The delay in revealing Brian's whereabouts, the carefully orchestrated timing of their statements, and the carefully chosen words they used only served to deepen the suspicion surrounding their role in the unfolding tragedy.

The subsequent search for Brian Laundrie, which captivated the nation for weeks, became a harrowing game of cat and mouse. Law enforcement, aided by an army of volunteers and fueled by relentless media coverage, combed through vast swathes of the Carlton Reserve, a sprawling wilderness area in Florida. The reserve, a labyrinthine network of trails, swamps, and dense vegetation, presented a formidable challenge, providing ample opportunity for someone determined to evade capture. The search stretched over several weeks, escalating from a targeted investigation to a wide-ranging, intensely public manhunt. The images broadcast across news channels—heavily equipped law enforcement officers slogging through swampy terrain, cadaver dogs sniffing the air, drones hovering overhead—painted a visceral picture of the extensive efforts being deployed.

The search itself became a source of intense public debate, with criticisms leveled at law enforcement's handling of the situation. Questions were raised about the allocation of resources, the strategies employed, and the overall effectiveness of the search. The public scrutiny, fueled by the 24/7 news cycle, intensified the pressure on investigators, demanding results and fostering a climate of heightened anxiety. The search highlighted the complexities of finding a fugitive in a vast, inhospitable environment, underscoring the challenges law enforcement faces in such scenarios.

While the search team focused on the Carlton Reserve, a parallel investigation continued, meticulously piecing together the events leading up to Gabby's death and Laundrie's subsequent actions. The examination of his financial records, his digital footprint, and his communications with family and friends revealed a pattern of carefully orchestrated deception. His withdrawals from Gabby's bank account, the timing of his purchases, and his movements after her disappearance all pointed towards a premeditated attempt to cover his tracks and escape the consequences of his actions.

The evidence uncovered during this period painted a chilling picture of a calculated attempt to mislead investigators. Laundrie's actions were not those of a panicked young man whose girlfriend had unexpectedly vanished; they were the deliberate actions of an individual determined to avoid accountability. His silence, his evasiveness, and his meticulous attempts to destroy evidence all contributed to the impression of a highly calculated strategy, a deliberate attempt to evade capture and obfuscate the truth. The meticulous nature of his actions, the strategic choices he made, indicated a level of premeditation and planning that went far beyond the impulsive act of a person overwhelmed by grief or remorse.

The discovery of Laundrie's personal belongings, including a notebook containing his confession, brought the agonizing search to a tragic conclusion. His handwritten confession provided a harrowing account of the events leading up to Gabby's death, detailing his actions and admitting to her murder. The details contained within the notebook, while deeply disturbing, provided law enforcement with the final pieces of the puzzle, confirming their suspicions and offering a grimly conclusive end to the investigation. The notebook entries revealed a level of premeditation and emotional detachment that shocked many, exposing a darker side to a story that had already captured the nation's attention.

The aftermath of the investigation resulted in a profound wave of public reflection and widespread condemnation. Laundrie's actions, meticulously planned and executed, underscored the dangers of domestic abuse and the insidious nature of manipulative relationships. The case served as a tragic illustration of how carefully constructed public personas can mask deeply troubled relationships. The seemingly idyllic social media portrayals of Gabby and Brian's road trip stood in stark contrast to the darker reality of the relationship revealed through witness accounts, Gabby's journal entries, and ultimately, Brian Laundrie's confession.

The investigation also highlighted the challenges faced by law enforcement in navigating the complexities of modern investigations. The reliance on digital evidence, the challenges of coordinating multiple investigative agencies, and the intense pressure exerted by the public and the media all underscored the complexities of solving a crime in the digital age. The case became a case study in the use of technology in both committing and solving crimes, highlighting both the opportunities and challenges presented by the digital world. The integration of various forms of evidence—digital footprints, eyewitness testimonies, physical evidence—demonstrated the necessity of a holistic investigative approach, a collaborative effort to piece together a complex and tragic narrative.

The Gabby Petito and Brian Laundrie case continues to resonate, serving as a stark reminder of the ever-present dangers of domestic violence, the importance of seeking help, and the need for a more comprehensive understanding of the complex dynamics of abusive relationships. The story remains a cautionary tale, a tragic testament to the hidden dangers that can lurk beneath the surface of seemingly idyllic relationships. It serves as a somber reminder of the profound impact of domestic violence and the need for continued efforts in prevention, intervention, and support for victims. Ultimately, the meticulous reconstruction of the events, the piecing together of seemingly disparate pieces of information, revealed not just a crime, but a chilling glimpse into the psychology of a perpetrator and the enduring impact of a tragedy that captivated a nation.

Chapter Three

The Investigation

A Race Against Time

The Search for Gabby Public Pressure and Police Strategy

The initial search for Gabby Petito was a frantic scramble, a race against time fueled by the chilling uncertainty surrounding her disappearance. The vastness of the search area, encompassing sprawling national parks and encompassing multiple states, immediately presented a significant logistical hurdle. The investigation, initially handled by local authorities in Grand Teton National Park, quickly escalated into a multi-agency effort, requiring seamless coordination between different law enforcement jurisdictions. The FBI, alongside state and local police forces, were tasked with combing through a landscape of immense scale, facing the challenge of effectively deploying limited resources across a geographically dispersed area.

The search strategy involved a combination of ground searches, aerial surveillance, and the deployment of specialized units. Teams of officers, often assisted by search and rescue personnel and volunteers, painstakingly traversed trails, combed through dense vegetation, and explored remote areas of the park. Helicopters and drones provided aerial support, scanning the landscape for any signs of Gabby, her belongings, or any other clues that might lead investigators to her whereabouts. Cadaver dogs, specially trained to detect the scent of decomposing human remains, played a critical role, systematically sniffing out potential areas of interest.

The sheer scale of the operation was unprecedented, the sheer volume of land requiring an efficient and coordinated strategy. The challenges of navigating the rugged terrain—steep inclines, dense forests, and unpredictable weather conditions—added another layer of complexity. The physical demands on search teams were immense, requiring stamina, resilience, and meticulous attention to detail. The intense pressure to find Gabby quickly, fueled by mounting public pressure and the growing media frenzy, compounded the already considerable challenges facing investigators.

The coordination between various law enforcement agencies proved crucial, requiring a seamless exchange of information and a unified command structure. Regular briefings and daily updates ensured that all teams were working from the same intelligence, maximizing efficiency and minimizing duplication of efforts. However, the logistical challenges of coordinating multiple agencies, often with differing protocols and jurisdictions, were considerable. Establishing effective communication lines, sharing real-time intelligence, and ensuring the smooth flow of information among various teams proved to be a complex undertaking.

The public's involvement in the search was both a boon and a burden. The outpouring of support, with hundreds of volunteers offering their assistance, provided a significant boost to the search effort. However, the massive influx of volunteers also required careful management to ensure safety, efficiency, and the coordinated deployment of resources. The sheer number of volunteers, coupled with the vastness of the search area, required a careful planning and coordination strategy to avoid compromising the investigation or endangering volunteers.

The media coverage played a crucial role in shaping public perception and influencing the course of the investigation. The 24/7 news cycle created a constant barrage of updates, speculation, and commentary. While this media attention generated public interest, it also exerted enormous pressure on investigators, often amplifying public anxiety and fostering a climate of heightened speculation. The need to balance the public's right to information with the need to protect the integrity of the investigation presented a delicate challenge.

Furthermore, the intense public scrutiny of the investigation brought its own set of complexities. The constant stream of updates, often based on incomplete or unverified information, sometimes hampered the investigative process, creating a difficult balancing act for law enforcement. The pressure to deliver quick results, fueled by the media's insatiable appetite for information, created a challenging environment for investigators working under tremendous pressure. The constant speculation and public commentary created a high-stakes atmosphere, where every decision and action were subject to intense scrutiny.

The initial search phase, while ultimately successful in locating Gabby's remains, served as a stark reminder of the challenges involved in large-scale searches, especially in remote and challenging terrains. The collaboration between agencies, the management of public support, and the need to navigate the intense media coverage all contributed to the complexities of the investigation. The experience provided valuable lessons in coordination, resource allocation, and public communication during high-stakes investigations.

The discovery of Gabby's body in Grand Teton National Park, tragically confirming the worst fears, marked a significant shift in the focus of the investigation. The transition from a missing person case to a homicide inquiry dramatically altered the investigative strategy, shifting the emphasis towards identifying the perpetrator and establishing the circumstances of the death. This change required a significant reallocation of resources and a recalibration of investigative priorities.

The transition required a seamless handover of information and a coordinated effort among federal, state, and local agencies involved. The FBI's expertise in large-scale crime investigations became crucial, and their resources were swiftly deployed to support local law enforcement agencies. Their deep experience in coordinating multi-agency investigations proved indispensable, ensuring a unified strategy and facilitating the efficient flow of information across jurisdictions.

The shift in focus also brought about a significant change in the public's perception of the case. The initial outpouring of concern and hope was replaced by grief and outrage. The public's attention turned towards Brian Laundrie, who had returned home from the road trip without Gabby, becoming the prime suspect in the eyes of the public and law enforcement. His silence and refusal to cooperate with investigators significantly amplified the public's suspicion.

The investigative teams turned their attention to meticulous reconstruction of the events leading up to Gabby's death. This involved analyzing Gabby's and Brian's social media activity, scrutinizing their financial records, and gathering statements from any witnesses who had interacted with the couple during their travels. The digital footprint of both Gabby and Brian became a critical source of evidence, offering a glimpse into their relationship dynamics and their activities before Gabby's disappearance. Investigators carefully examined GPS data from their phones, analyzed credit card transactions, and examined their social media posts, meticulously reconstructing their movements and interactions during their trip.

The investigation extended beyond the immediate physical evidence, delving into the psychological aspects of the relationship between Gabby and Brian. Investigators studied Gabby's journal entries and her communications with friends and family, gaining insights into the dynamics of their relationship and possible signs of abuse or control. The information gleaned from these sources provided a valuable context for understanding the circumstances surrounding Gabby's death. The examination of their digital communications, especially text messages and social media exchanges, illuminated the relationship's complexities, revealing subtle signs of conflict and control that had previously remained hidden.

The intense media scrutiny played a significant role throughout the investigation. While the media provided critical information to the public, it also generated intense pressure on investigators. The 24/7 news cycle created an atmosphere of constant speculation, with every detail of the case magnified and scrutinized. This presented challenges for investigators working under intense public and media pressure. The need to maintain the integrity of the investigation while simultaneously keeping the public informed presented a delicate balancing act.

As the investigation progressed, the public's demand for justice intensified. Gabby's family, advocating for transparency and accountability, publicly urged Brian Laundrie to cooperate. The unwavering support and pressure from Gabby's family played a significant role in propelling the investigation forward. Their advocacy served as a powerful catalyst for maintaining public focus on the case and demanding answers.

In conclusion, the investigation into Gabby Petito's death was a complex and multifaceted undertaking. It involved the collaboration of multiple agencies, navigating the challenges of a vast search area and intense media scrutiny. The process highlighted the importance of efficient coordination, meticulous evidence gathering, and a nuanced understanding of the psychological dynamics at play. The tragic loss of Gabby Petito served as a wake-up call, underscoring the pervasive issue of domestic violence and the need for heightened awareness and more robust protective measures.

The Role of Social Media Citizen Detectives and Misinformation

The digital age, with its omnipresent social media platforms, presented a unique and often paradoxical challenge to the investigation into Gabby Petito's disappearance and subsequent murder. While the internet, and specifically social media, became a crucial tool for disseminating information and garnering public support, it also became a breeding ground for speculation, misinformation, and even outright harassment. This created a double-edged sword, simultaneously accelerating the investigation while simultaneously hindering its progress.

The initial days of Gabby's disappearance saw a flurry of activity on platforms like Instagram, Facebook, and Twitter. Gabby's carefully curated Instagram feed, showcasing a seemingly idyllic van-life adventure, starkly contrasted with the growing fear and uncertainty surrounding her disappearance. This juxtaposition fueled intense public interest and concern, prompting a surge in online discussions, hashtag campaigns (Find-GabbyPetito), and the rapid dissemination of crucial information, such as photographs, videos, and details about her last known location. The sheer volume of shares, comments, and retweets amplified the case's visibility exponentially, pushing it beyond the confines of local news and attracting national, then international, attention. This unprecedented level of public engagement, spurred by social media, undoubtedly played a significant role in accelerating the initial search efforts.

Citizen detectives, armed with their smartphones and internet access, emerged as a significant force in the investigation. Many individuals, independently scouring social media posts, photographs, and videos of Gabby and Brian's travels, pieced together timelines, identified potential witnesses, and even pinpointed locations featured in their social media content. Their online sleuthing, often involving painstakingly analyzing seemingly insignificant details—a particular license plate number glimpsed in a background, a specific geographical feature visible in a photograph—proved surprisingly effective. In some cases, these amateur investigators provided law enforcement with critical leads that might otherwise have remained undiscovered. For example, the detailed mapping of the couple's movements, gleaned from geolocation data embedded in their social media posts and photographs, helped investigators narrow down the search areas and prioritize their efforts.

This collaboration between citizen detectives and law enforcement, although unprecedented in its scale, wasn't without its complexities. The information shared online, while sometimes invaluable, was often unverified and potentially unreliable. Rumors, speculation, and outright misinformation spread rapidly, sometimes overshadowing accurate information and creating confusion for investigators. The challenge for law enforcement was to sift through the vast ocean of online information, separating credible leads from unsubstantiated claims and outright fabrications. The speed and scale of the online discourse made this a daunting task, requiring a dedicated team to monitor and analyze social media activity. The potential for inaccurate information to derail the investigation was real, highlighting the need for careful verification and rigorous fact-checking.

The intense media scrutiny fueled by social media further complicated the investigation. The 24/7 news cycle, fueled by a constant stream of online updates and speculation, created an environment of intense pressure for law enforcement. Every detail of the case was magnified and scrutinized, with every investigative action, or perceived inaction, attracting criticism and commentary. This constant public pressure created challenges, forcing investigators to balance the need for transparency with the imperative to protect the integrity of the ongoing investigation. The need for carefully managed information releases, strategically calibrated to both address public concerns and avoid jeopardizing investigative leads, was paramount.

Furthermore, the online frenzy surrounding the case inevitably led to the harassment of individuals connected to Brian Laundrie. Family members, friends, and even acquaintances became targets of online abuse, with their social media accounts bombarded with hateful messages, threats, and unwarranted accusations. The anonymity and reach of social media provided a shield for those perpetrating such harassment, making it difficult for law enforcement to effectively intervene and protect individuals from unwarranted online attacks. This underscored the dark side of citizen involvement, demonstrating how the passionate desire for justice could sometimes spill over into inappropriate, unethical, and even illegal behavior. The line between assisting the investigation and engaging in harmful online actions became blurred.

Social media also amplified the discussion surrounding domestic violence and its prevalence. Gabby's seemingly idyllic online persona, contrasted with the tragic reality of her situation, became a poignant symbol of the often-hidden nature of abusive relationships. The online conversation spurred a renewed focus on identifying the signs of domestic abuse, providing support for victims, and encouraging individuals to seek help when needed. The widespread sharing of information and resources on domestic violence awareness, facilitated by social media, served as a positive outcome of the tragic case. It fostered important discussions regarding the importance of healthy relationships and the available resources for victims of abuse.

In conclusion, social media played a complex and multifaceted role in the investigation into Gabby Petito's death. It served as both a valuable tool for investigators and a source of misinformation and harassment. The rapid dissemination of information, the emergence of citizen detectives, and the heightened public awareness of domestic violence were all positive aspects of social media's influence. However, the spread of rumors, the pressure exerted on law enforcement, and the harassment of those connected to Brian Laundrie illustrated the inherent risks and ethical challenges presented by online participation in criminal investigations. The Gabby Petito case serves as a cautionary tale highlighting both the powerful potential and the considerable pitfalls of the digital age's influence on true crime investigations. It underscores the need for responsible online engagement, the careful verification of information, and the protection of individuals from the harmful effects of unchecked online activity. The case serves as a vital case study for law enforcement, emphasizing the need to develop strategies to manage the flow of online information, leverage its beneficial aspects, and mitigate its potential harms.

The Forensic Evidence Unraveling the Truth

The discovery of Gabby Petito's body in the vast expanse of Bridger-Teton National Forest marked a pivotal moment, shifting the investigation from a missing person case to a homicide. The subsequent forensic analysis would become crucial in unraveling the sequence of events leading to her tragic death and ultimately building a compelling case against Brian Laundrie. The meticulous work of the forensic teams, combining traditional investigative techniques with cutting-edge digital forensics, provided a chillingly detailed account of Gabby's final hours and the events preceding her death.

The autopsy report, released by the Teton County Coroner's Office, provided the first definitive insights into Gabby's cause of death. The report detailed the injuries sustained, confirming manual strangulation as the cause of death. This conclusion, based on both external and internal examinations, laid the groundwork for the prosecution's case, establishing the violent nature of Gabby's demise and supporting the theory of intentional homicide. The specific details, carefully documented in the report, were crucial in helping investigators piece together the chronology of the events leading up to her death. The absence of any other contributing factors to her death pointed directly to the intentional action of another individual. The precise nature of the injuries, described clinically yet powerfully in the report, painted a grim picture of the final moments of Gabby's life, highlighting the brutality of the attack.

Beyond the immediate cause of death, the autopsy provided other crucial clues. The time of death estimation, a complex calculation based on various factors including post-mortem changes, was crucial in establishing a timeline for the investigation. This timeline, subsequently corroborated by other evidence, helped investigators focus their efforts on specific time periods and locations. For instance, the estimated time of death allowed law enforcement to refine their search for potential witnesses, focusing on those who may have been in the vicinity of the crime scene around that time. The precise location of the body, within the vast national forest, also provided valuable information to investigators, potentially revealing details about the manner in which Gabby's body was transported and disposed of. Any trace evidence collected from the body itself, such as fibers or other materials, could potentially link her to specific locations or individuals. The autopsy report, while a somber document, was undeniably a cornerstone of the forensic investigation, offering vital clues to the narrative of Gabby's murder.

The crime scene itself, the remote location in Wyoming where Gabby's body was found, provided a wealth of forensic evidence, though the harsh environmental conditions presented considerable challenges. The investigators meticulously documented the scene, carefully collecting any potential evidence. This involved a detailed photographic record, creating a comprehensive visual record of the environment and Gabby's position. The terrain, vegetation, and any unusual features of the location were carefully documented. This painstaking work was crucial not just for the immediate investigation but also for potential future legal proceedings.

The collection of physical evidence was a high priority. Soil samples were collected from around the body and compared to samples taken from other locations where Gabby and Brian were known to have been, potentially helping to reconstruct their movements in the days leading up to her death. Any fibers, hairs, or other microscopic debris found near the body were collected and analyzed. These seemingly insignificant items could potentially link the crime scene to specific vehicles or individuals, offering vital links in the chain of evidence. The thorough documentation and collection of this physical evidence in the challenging environmental conditions underscored the dedication and expertise of the forensic team involved. The methodical approach ensured that no potential piece of evidence, however small or seemingly insignificant, was overlooked.

Digital forensics played an equally critical role in the investigation, providing insight into the couple's movements, communications, and online activity. The analysis of Gabby and Brian's cell phones, computers, and social media accounts provided a digital trail of their journey, mapping their movements across the country and offering critical clues about their interactions in the weeks leading up to Gabby's death. Geolocation data embedded in photos and videos posted on social media proved invaluable in retracing their route, identifying potential witnesses along the way and helping investigators to build a comprehensive timeline of their travels. The content of their online communication, particularly text messages and social media posts, revealed a pattern of escalating conflict and tension within their relationship, providing valuable insight into the dynamics that ultimately contributed to the tragedy. This digital evidence, meticulously pieced together by forensic specialists, provided a vital context for the physical evidence found at the crime scene and in the autopsy report.

Analyzing the couple's cell phone data presented a complex challenge for investigators, involving careful extraction and interpretation of deleted files, geolocation data, and communication records. The challenges of extracting data from damaged or compromised devices were overcome through the use of specialized techniques, demonstrating the advanced capabilities of modern digital forensics. The digital trail, although fragmented at times, ultimately provided a compelling narrative of the couple's journey, highlighting points of contention and escalating conflict. The messages exchanged, though sometimes cryptic or seemingly inconsequential on their own, revealed a pattern of increasing tension and emotional distress.

The vehicle itself, the white Ford Transit van the couple was traveling in, became a crucial piece of the forensic puzzle. A thorough search of the van uncovered potential traces of evidence, such as bloodstains, fibers, or other materials, which were carefully collected and analyzed. The vehicle's GPS data, if intact, could have offered additional confirmation of the couple's movements and locations. Even subtle traces of evidence, such as hair or fibers found within the vehicle's interior, could provide valuable connections between the individuals and the locations they visited.

The vehicle's condition, both interior and exterior, was carefully documented, with photographs and detailed notes providing a record of its state upon discovery. The meticulous examination of the van proved an essential step in confirming or challenging various aspects of the narrative constructed through other forms of evidence.

The forensic evidence, painstakingly collected and analyzed, formed a compelling narrative, piecing together the tragedy of Gabby Petito's death. The combination of autopsy results, crime scene analysis, and digital forensics created a powerful case, establishing the timeline of events, identifying the cause of death, and providing vital clues about the circumstances surrounding the murder. The synergy between traditional investigative methods and the latest digital forensics techniques underscored the power of modern criminal investigation and the importance of interdisciplinary collaboration in solving complex cases. The forensic findings, while undoubtedly tragic, served as the bedrock upon which justice would be sought. The meticulous and comprehensive nature of the forensic work not only helped to solve the case but also provided a profound understanding of the complexities involved in such investigations, emphasizing the importance of scientific rigour and detail-oriented analysis in achieving justice. The case serves as a stark reminder of the devastating consequences of unchecked violence and the crucial role of forensic science in seeking accountability.

The Legal Process Challenges and Outcomes

The discovery of Gabby Petito's remains shifted the focus from a missing person investigation to a full-blown homicide inquiry, triggering a complex legal process that would test the limits of law enforcement and the judicial system. Brian Laundrie, initially a person of interest, quickly became the prime suspect, fueling an intense manhunt and a nationwide media frenzy. The legal strategy, from both the prosecution's and the defense's perspectives (had Laundrie lived to face trial), would have hinged on effectively presenting and refuting the mountain of evidence painstakingly gathered during the investigation.

The charges filed against Laundrie, had he been apprehended alive, would have been predicated on the forensic evidence detailed in the autopsy report and the circumstantial evidence gathered from the crime scene, the couple's van, and their digital footprints. The prosecution would have had to prove beyond a reasonable doubt that Laundrie caused Gabby's death and the manner in which it occurred. This involved presenting the autopsy findings—the cause of death (manual strangulation), the manner of death (homicide), and the estimated time of death—as irrefutable evidence of a violent act. They would likely have focused on demonstrating a clear pattern of escalating domestic violence in the relationship, drawing on witness testimonies (if available), digital communications, and the physical evidence found in the van to support the narrative of a premeditated murder. The location of Gabby's body, the remote and secluded nature of the crime scene, would have likely been used to suggest Laundrie's intent to conceal the crime and evade capture.

The defense, hypothetically, would have faced an uphill battle. Given the overwhelming evidence against Laundrie, any plausible defense strategy would likely have revolved around challenging the prosecution's interpretation of the evidence. They might have attempted to create reasonable doubt by questioning the reliability of certain pieces of evidence, perhaps arguing that the chain of custody had been compromised, or raising questions about the accuracy of the forensic analysis. Another line of defense might have involved attempting to cast doubt on the prosecution's portrayal of the relationship as one of escalating abuse, perhaps arguing that Gabby and Brian had an argument that tragically resulted in an accidental death. However, the strength of the physical and digital evidence—the autopsy report, the crime scene analysis, the digital communications—would have made this a difficult, if not impossible, task. Furthermore, the timeline, meticulously reconstructed through forensic investigation, would have left little room for alternative explanations of the events leading up to Gabby's death.

Beyond the specific charges, the case raised complex legal questions surrounding domestic violence and the challenges of prosecuting such cases. The prosecution would have had to navigate the legal complexities of proving domestic abuse in the absence of direct witnesses to the altercation. This would have relied heavily on demonstrating a pattern of abusive behavior through indirect evidence, such as text messages, social media posts, and witness statements from individuals who had observed the couple's interactions. Moreover, the geographic scope of the investigation—spanning multiple states and encompassing both physical and digital evidence—would have presented significant logistical and jurisdictional challenges. Gathering evidence from various agencies and jurisdictions would have required careful coordination and collaboration between law enforcement, forensic teams, and legal professionals.

The legal proceedings themselves would have unfolded within the framework of the judicial system, subject to its established processes and procedures. Pre-trial motions, evidence discovery, witness testimonies, and the eventual presentation of the case to a jury would have followed a carefully orchestrated sequence. The prosecution would have had the burden of proving Laundrie's guilt beyond a reasonable doubt, a high standard that necessitates presenting irrefutable evidence to a jury. The defense, even facing a seemingly insurmountable mountain of evidence, would have been afforded all the rights and protections guaranteed by the legal system.

The challenges of prosecuting a domestic violence case are often profound. Victims rarely report abuse, making it challenging to compile a record of abuse. Evidence is often circumstantial, based on patterns of behavior and statements from the victim. In cases where the victim is deceased, the burden of proof rests entirely on the evidence gathered post-mortem, which can be both extensive and highly complex, as in this instance.

The outcome of the case, considering Laundrie's suicide, remains tragically inconclusive in terms of a formal legal verdict. While the weight of the forensic evidence strongly suggests Laundrie's guilt, the lack of a trial prevented a formal adjudication of culpability. This lack of a trial left a lingering sense of incompleteness, denying Gabby Petito's family the satisfaction of a full legal reckoning.

However, the comprehensive investigation, even without a courtroom trial, shed light on the devastating consequences of domestic violence and provided a powerful case study of the investigative tools and legal strategies utilized in prosecuting similar offenses. The detailed documentation of the case served as a critical resource for future legal professionals, offering valuable insights into handling complex domestic violence homicides. This comprehensive approach ensures that despite the tragic circumstances, lessons learned from the Gabby Petito case will ultimately improve future investigations and prosecutions, aiding in bringing perpetrators to justice and preventing future tragedies. The extensive documentation also served as a testament to the dedication of law enforcement agencies and forensic scientists involved in seeking justice for Gabby Petito, emphasizing the importance of rigorous investigation and the power of collaboration in unraveling complex criminal cases.

The absence of a trial, though, highlights the limitations of the legal system in offering complete closure in such cases. While the overwhelming evidence pointed to Laundrie's guilt, the lack of a formal conviction leaves a profound sense of unease, underscoring the challenges faced when a perpetrator evades legal accountability through self-inflicted death. The case, despite its tragic conclusion, has spurred conversations about domestic violence awareness, the resources available to victims, and the importance of recognizing the signs of an abusive relationship. It served as a powerful catalyst for legislative reforms and increased funding for programs aimed at supporting survivors of domestic violence. Moreover, the meticulous reporting of the case and the extensive forensic analysis served as a valuable learning experience for law enforcement agencies, forensic scientists, and legal professionals, informing future investigative strategies and enhancing the ability to effectively prosecute domestic violence cases. Gabby Petito's story, though devastating, has had a far-reaching impact, pushing the boundaries of domestic violence awareness and influencing legal and policy changes to protect future victims. The legacy of this tragedy serves as a stark reminder of the need for continuous vigilance and ongoing efforts to combat domestic violence.

The Aftermath A Community Grieves

The quiet town of North Port, Florida, Brian Laundrie's home, became a focal point of intense media scrutiny. The normally peaceful streets were suddenly swarming with journalists, satellite trucks, and curious onlookers, transforming the familiar landscape into a stage for a national tragedy. The Laundrie family home, once a symbol of suburban normalcy, became a symbol of suspicion and grief, its front yard a makeshift memorial—a testament to the community's conflicted emotions. While some sympathized with the family's loss, many others felt anger and frustration, fueled by the unanswered questions surrounding Gabby's death and the perceived lack of cooperation from the Laundries. This tension created a palpable atmosphere of unease and distrust within the community, fracturing the usual social fabric. The neighbors, many of whom had known the Laundries for years, found themselves caught in a maelstrom of public opinion, forced to navigate complex emotions of sympathy, anger, and fear. Some spoke out publicly, offering their perspectives and experiences, while others chose to remain silent, seeking to shield themselves from the intense media scrutiny.

The impact extended far beyond North Port. Gabby Petito's death resonated deeply with communities across the nation, touching upon a collective anxiety surrounding domestic violence and the vulnerability of young women. Social media platforms exploded with discussions, debates, and tributes. The hashtag JusticeForGabby became a rallying cry, amplifying calls for accountability and prompting widespread conversations about the prevalence of domestic abuse and the need for improved support systems for victims. The case became a lightning rod for discussions about the complexities of relationships, the manipulative tactics employed by abusers, and the importance of recognizing the signs of abusive behavior. The idyllic imagery of Gabby's carefully curated social media presence starkly contrasted with the horrifying reality of her final days, highlighting the performative nature of online personas and the dangers of overlooking the subtle indicators of domestic strife hidden behind carefully crafted digital facades. This contrast created a powerful narrative, effectively capturing public attention and sparking a nationwide dialogue about the unseen realities of many seemingly happy and successful relationships.

The outpouring of support for Gabby's family was immense, a testament to the public's empathy and collective grief. Fundraising campaigns generated substantial financial contributions to help with funeral expenses and legal costs. Memorial services were held across the country, drawing hundreds, if not thousands, of mourners who had never met Gabby but felt a profound sense of loss and outrage at her tragic demise. The media, initially criticized for its intense coverage, also played a role in amplifying the family's voice, ensuring their story was heard and their call for justice was amplified across the nation and beyond. This public display of support, although unable to reverse the tragedy, offered a measure of comfort and validation, showing the family they were not alone in their grief and that their daughter's death was not being ignored.

Yet, even within this wave of support, there existed a parallel current of controversy. The Laundrie family's silence and perceived lack of cooperation fueled public anger and suspicion. While their right to remain silent under the law was upheld, their actions were subjected to intense public scrutiny and condemnation. This created a complex dilemma, highlighting the conflict between individual rights and the community's need for answers and justice. The media's role in amplifying these conflicting sentiments became a subject of debate, raising important questions about responsible reporting and the ethical considerations of covering a tragedy of this magnitude. The balance between the family's grief, the public's demand for closure, and the media's responsibility to inform the public became a complex challenge, often met with inconsistent success.

The aftermath of the Gabby Petito case was not solely characterized by grief and outrage. It also ignited a significant wave of activism aimed at improving domestic violence awareness, prevention, and support systems. Advocacy groups saw a surge in donations, volunteers, and engagement, using the case to galvanize support for their initiatives. Existing legislation related to domestic violence was reviewed and debated, with calls for stronger protections for victims and harsher penalties for abusers. The case became a catalyst for policy changes, creating the momentum for more significant legislative action aimed at tackling the issue more effectively. This proactive response transformed a tragic loss into a powerful force for positive change, demonstrating the capacity of collective grief to fuel meaningful societal reforms.

However, the activism wasn't without its challenges. Navigating the complexities of legislative processes, securing funding for programs, and addressing the systemic issues that contribute to domestic violence required a sustained and coordinated effort. The initial wave of public attention, though significant, gradually subsided. Maintaining this momentum, ensuring lasting changes, and continuing to advocate for better support systems became a crucial long-term goal for activists, demanding consistent and determined engagement to avoid the all-too-familiar pattern of public interest waning after a tragedy fades from the headlines.

The legacy of Gabby Petito's case extends far beyond the immediate aftermath. Her story served as a stark reminder of the pervasiveness of domestic violence and the devastating consequences it can have. It underscored the importance of early intervention, improved support systems for victims, and effective legal mechanisms for prosecuting abusers. Educational campaigns were developed and implemented, focusing on recognizing the signs of abusive relationships and providing resources for victims seeking help. The case's impact on the landscape of domestic violence advocacy is undeniable, creating a lasting ripple effect that continues to shape the conversation and efforts aimed at prevention and intervention.

Furthermore, Gabby's case profoundly impacted the way law enforcement approaches missing person cases and domestic violence investigations. The swift and coordinated response, though ultimately unsuccessful in preventing the tragic outcome, highlighted the importance of inter-agency collaboration, comprehensive data analysis, and the utilization of advanced investigative techniques. The detailed forensic analysis conducted in the Petito-Laundrie case became a case study for training law enforcement personnel across the country. The lessons learned from the challenges encountered were used to refine investigative protocols, improve training programs, and enhance resource allocation. This post-case analysis proved to be a crucial element in ensuring that such tragedies are addressed more effectively in the future, transforming the experience of loss into a powerful catalyst for improved law enforcement practices.

In conclusion, the aftermath of Gabby Petito's death was a complex tapestry woven from threads of grief, outrage, activism, and legal and policy reform. The community's response, encompassing both the immediate outpouring of support and the subsequent wave of activism, served as a testament to the power of collective empathy and the determination to create positive change in the face of tragedy. While the absence of a trial denied the family complete legal closure, the far-reaching impact of the case serves as a powerful legacy, leaving an indelible mark on domestic violence awareness, advocacy, and legal processes. Gabby Petito's story, though deeply tragic, continues to inspire a renewed commitment to addressing domestic violence and preventing future tragedies. It stands as a stark reminder of the enduring need for ongoing vigilance, continuous advocacy, and unwavering support for those impacted by domestic abuse. Her legacy will continue to be felt in countless ways, shaping the conversation and driving efforts to combat a pervasive and insidious problem.

Chapter Four

The Psychological Control and Manipulation

Understanding Domestic Violence Patterns and Dynamics

The tragedy of Gabby Petito's murder illuminated not only the brutal reality of domestic violence but also the insidious psychology underpinning it. Understanding this psychology is crucial, not only to comprehend the events that led to her death but also to prevent future tragedies. Domestic violence is not simply a matter of physical aggression; it's a complex interplay of power, control, and manipulation, carefully orchestrated by the abuser to subjugate their victim.

One of the most pervasive tactics employed by abusers is the gradual erosion of their victim's self-esteem and independence. This process, often subtle and insidious, begins with seemingly innocuous comments or actions. The abuser might subtly criticize the victim's appearance, choices, or abilities, gradually chipping away at their confidence until they begin to doubt their own judgment and worth. This constant stream of negativity creates a climate of fear and uncertainty, making the victim increasingly reliant on the abuser for validation and approval. The victim's support network may be subtly undermined, with the abuser isolating them from friends and family, further strengthening their dependence and leaving them vulnerable to further abuse. This isolation can manifest in various ways – forbidding contact with loved ones, controlling access to communication devices (phones, computers), or simply making the victim feel guilty or ashamed for interacting with others.

This manipulation extends beyond verbal criticism. Abusers often employ what is known as "gaslighting," a manipulative tactic where they systematically distort reality, making the victim question their own sanity and perception. The abuser might deny events that occurred, twist words to shift blame, or create scenarios designed to confuse and disorient the victim. This psychological warfare can be incredibly damaging, leaving the victim feeling bewildered, fragile, and unable to trust their own instincts. They may begin to internalize the abuser's narrative, accepting the blame for the abuse and believing they are somehow at fault.

Control is the cornerstone of abusive relationships. This control extends to various facets of the victim's life, including their finances, social interactions, and even their daily routines. Financial control can be exerted through limiting access to funds, controlling bank accounts, or demanding complete financial transparency while withholding information about their own finances. This financial dependence makes it exceedingly difficult for the victim to leave the relationship, as they may lack the resources to support themselves independently. Similarly, control over social interactions isolates the victim from their support network, leaving them vulnerable and dependent on the abuser for companionship and emotional support. This control can be blatant – forbidding contact with friends and family – or more subtle, such as creating an atmosphere of intimidation that discourages the victim from socializing.

The abuser's control often manifests in controlling the victim's daily life, from determining what they wear and eat to dictating their schedule and movements. The victim's autonomy is progressively reduced, leaving them feeling trapped and powerless. This control often evolves gradually, starting with small restrictions that escalate over time, making it harder for the victim to recognize the extent of the manipulation until it's too late. The gradual nature of this control allows the abuser to maintain a veneer of normalcy, often making it difficult for outsiders to recognize the abusive dynamic.

Furthermore, cycles of abuse often characterize abusive relationships. These cycles typically consist of three phases: tension building, acute battering, and a period of remorse or contrition. During the tension-building phase, the abuser's behavior becomes increasingly erratic and unpredictable, often characterized by anger, irritability, and controlling behavior. The acute battering phase involves the actual act of violence, whether physical, verbal, emotional, or sexual. Following this, there's a period of remorse, where the abuser expresses regret, apologizes profusely, and promises to change their behavior. This period of remorse is crucial because it creates a false sense of hope, drawing the victim back into the relationship and making them believe that the abuse will never happen again. However, this is a cyclical pattern; the remorse is temporary, and the cycle eventually repeats itself, leaving the victim trapped in a never-ending loop of abuse and false hope.

The psychological manipulation involved in domestic violence is not simply a matter of individual personality flaws. Research in social psychology highlights the roles of power imbalances, societal norms, and learned behaviors in perpetuating abusive relationships. For instance, societal gender norms have historically normalized certain forms of male dominance and female subordination, creating an environment where some men feel entitled to control their female partners. Furthermore, the abuse may be learned behavior, reflecting patterns observed in the abuser's own upbringing or social environment.

Understanding these underlying psychological dynamics is essential for effectively addressing and preventing domestic violence. This understanding requires a multi-faceted approach that encompasses both individual-level interventions (such as therapy for both the abuser and the victim) and systemic changes (such as legislative reforms, improved law enforcement training, and enhanced social support systems). The focus should be on empowering victims to recognize the signs of abuse, to develop coping mechanisms, and to seek help from trusted resources. Simultaneously, efforts must be made to address the societal norms that contribute to the perpetuation of domestic violence and to hold abusers accountable for their actions.

The Gabby Petito case, while heartbreaking, serves as a stark reminder of the urgent need for widespread awareness and effective interventions. The seemingly idyllic image she presented on social media masked a disturbing reality, highlighting the importance of recognizing the subtle signs of abuse that can often be hidden behind a carefully crafted public persona. Her story underscores the need for increased education and awareness, not only among potential victims but also among friends, family members, and community members who might play a vital role in identifying and reporting cases of domestic violence.

The legal system also plays a critical role. While the legal process can sometimes feel slow and frustrating, effective legal intervention can offer protection for victims and hold abusers accountable. The shortcomings of the legal response in some cases highlight the ongoing need to improve training and collaboration among law enforcement agencies, prosecutors, and social service organizations. Furthermore, legal frameworks must be strengthened to provide greater protection for victims, to ensure that their safety is prioritized, and that the justice system effectively addresses the complexities of domestic violence cases.

Finally, the long-term consequences of domestic violence extend far beyond the immediate physical and emotional trauma. Victims may experience lasting mental health issues, such as PTSD, anxiety, and depression. Children exposed to domestic violence often suffer long-term developmental, emotional, and psychological consequences. Addressing the lasting impact of domestic violence requires comprehensive support systems, including access to mental health services, economic support, and safe housing for victims and their children.

The pervasive nature and devastating consequences of domestic violence necessitate a multi-pronged approach that addresses both the individual and systemic factors that contribute to it. The tragedy of Gabby Petito's case serves as a powerful catalyst for change, highlighting the importance of increased awareness, improved support systems, and a strengthened commitment to justice and accountability. Only through a sustained effort toward prevention, intervention, and support can we hope to prevent future tragedies and create a society where domestic violence is no longer tolerated. Her story demands that we not only mourn her loss but also learn from it, striving to create a world where such tragedies are a thing of the past.

The Cycle of Abuse Identifying Warning Signs

The insidious nature of domestic abuse often lies in its cyclical pattern, a repetitive dance of escalating tension, violent outbursts, and fleeting remorse that traps victims in a web of fear and false hope. Understanding this cycle is crucial for recognizing and escaping abusive relationships. It's not a simple progression; rather, it's a complex interplay of psychological manipulation and learned behaviors, subtly weaving itself into the fabric of a relationship until the victim's sense of self is completely eroded.

The first phase, the tension-building phase, is often characterized by a gradual increase in the abuser's controlling behaviors. This might manifest as increased criticism, subtle put-downs designed to undermine the victim's self-esteem, or controlling actions disguised as concern. The abuser might start monitoring the victim's phone calls or social media activity, questioning their whereabouts, or dictating their clothing choices.

These seemingly minor actions create an atmosphere of suspicion and anxiety, slowly constricting the victim's freedom and independence. The victim might start to self-censor, avoiding certain topics of conversation or altering their behavior to appease the abuser. Friends and family might observe a change in the victim's demeanor, noticing a growing withdrawal from social activities or a hesitancy to share details about their relationship. This phase is insidious because it often goes unnoticed, or dismissed as minor disagreements. The escalation is so gradual that the victim may not recognize the pattern of abuse until it's firmly entrenched.

Consider the subtle ways this control can manifest: a constant barrage of text messages demanding updates on the victim's location; a casual remark that makes the victim question their own judgment; a subtle change in financial arrangements, with the abuser gaining greater control over shared accounts. These actions, while seemingly insignificant in isolation, are deliberate steps in a larger pattern of control. The tension builds slowly, like a pressure cooker nearing its boiling point, until the inevitable explosion.

The second phase, the acute battering phase, marks the peak of the cycle. This phase can involve physical violence, but it is not limited to it. It encompasses a wide range of abusive behaviors, including verbal assaults, threats, intimidation, sexual coercion, and emotional manipulation. This phase is the most visible and frightening, but its significance lies in the context of the preceding tension-building phase. The violence is not random; it's the culmination of a carefully orchestrated pattern of control and intimidation. The abuser may feel justified in their actions, believing that the victim provoked the outburst or that their controlling behaviors are necessary to maintain order in the relationship. The aftermath of this phase is often characterized by intense emotional distress for the victim, leaving them feeling confused, traumatized, and isolated. The experience can be physically and psychologically devastating, leaving lasting scars.

The aftermath of the acute battering phase is pivotal: the period of remorse or contrition. This phase, often described as the"honeymoon phase," is characterized by the abuser's profuse apologies, promises of change, and expressions of remorse. The abuser might shower the victim with gifts, attention, and affection, creating a false sense of hope and security. This is a crucial part of the cycle, as it reinforces the victim's dependence on the abuser and prevents them from leaving the relationship. The abuser's remorse is often genuine, at least temporarily, but it's not a genuine change of behavior. Rather, it's a tactical maneuver designed to maintain control and ensure that the cycle repeats itself. The victim, exhausted and emotionally drained, may find it difficult to resist the abuser's charm and promises, believing that things will be different this time. This hope is often misplaced; the cycle, once established, continues to repeat itself, each time becoming more intense and destructive.

This cyclical pattern is rarely linear. The stages may overlap, or the length of each phase may vary. The tension-building phase might be prolonged, while the acute battering phase is relatively short. The remorse phase might be superficial and fleeting, lasting only until the next cycle begins. The victim may become increasingly desensitized to the violence, while simultaneously becoming more hyper-vigilant, anticipating the next outburst. The unpredictability is a powerful tool of control, keeping the victim in a constant state of fear and uncertainty.

Recognizing the warning signs of this cycle is critical, not only for the victim but also for friends, family, and loved ones who might observe concerning behaviors. Early intervention can prevent escalation and offer support to those caught in abusive relationships. These warning signs might include isolation from friends and family; controlling behaviors; constant criticism and put-downs; frequent outbursts of anger; threats of violence or harm; financial control; gaslighting; and manipulation. The signs are often subtle, masked by moments of affection and remorse. It is crucial to look for patterns of behavior, rather than focusing on individual incidents. A single act of violence is alarming, but a pattern of controlling behaviors, escalating tension, and cycles of abuse points to a far more serious problem

Escape from this cycle is rarely easy. The victim often faces significant challenges, including financial dependence, fear of retaliation, lack of support, and the internalized belief that they are somehow at fault. The abuser's manipulation has often eroded their self-esteem and independence, making it difficult for them to believe they deserve better or that they have the strength to leave. Seeking help is crucial, and there are numerous resources available, including domestic violence shelters, support groups, and counseling services. These resources offer a lifeline, providing safe spaces, emotional support, and practical assistance in escaping the cycle of abuse and rebuilding their lives.

The Gabby Petito case serves as a tragic reminder of the devastating consequences of unchecked abuse. It underscores the importance of recognizing the warning signs and taking action to intervene. The apparent perfection of her social media presence masked a far more sinister reality, highlighting the deception often present in abusive relationships. Her story demands that we remain vigilant, educating ourselves and others about the signs of domestic violence, and supporting those who are trapped in abusive cycles. It is a call to action, urging us to create a society where such tragedies are not only prevented but are rendered unthinkable. The cycle of abuse is a dark and complex phenomenon, but with increased awareness, support, and intervention, we can work toward breaking its grip and empowering victims to reclaim their lives. The fight against domestic violence requires a collective effort, one that demands understanding, empathy, and unwavering commitment to justice and safety.

Gaslighting and Manipulation Brian Laundries Tactics

Brian Laundrie's actions, while chillingly apparent in retrospect, were masterfully disguised during the unfolding events of Gabby Petito's disappearance and death. He employed a complex tapestry of gaslighting and manipulation techniques, woven so subtly into the fabric of their relationship that they went largely unnoticed until the tragic consequences became irrefutable. Understanding these tactics, through the lens of established psychological frameworks, unveils a disturbing picture of calculated control and emotional abuse.

One of the most potent tools in Laundrie's arsenal was the deliberate erosion of Petito's self-esteem. This insidious process didn't involve overt aggression; rather, it was a slow, methodical chipping away at her confidence, subtly undermining her sense of self-worth and judgment. This is a classic gaslighting technique: making the victim question their own sanity and perception of reality. Small, seemingly insignificant comments – a dismissive "You're overreacting," a sarcastic "Are you sure about that?", a subtle rolling of the eyes – accumulated over time, creating a constant undercurrent of doubt. These micro-aggressions planted seeds of insecurity, making Petito increasingly dependent on Laundrie for validation and approval. Her increasingly frequent requests for reassurance and validation, documented in texts and calls with family and friends, highlight the success of Laundrie's subtle yet devastating manipulation. He subtly shifted the narrative, consistently positioning himself as the reasonable, calm party, while painting Petito as emotionally unstable and prone to exaggeration. This carefully constructed narrative served to isolate Petito, making it harder for her to seek help or confide in others.

The nature of their relationship, documented through social media posts and recovered text messages, paints a picture of a power imbalance increasingly skewed in Laundrie's favor. The meticulously crafted Instagram posts depicting a happy couple on an idyllic road trip stand in stark contrast to the reality revealed by police investigations and witness accounts. This performative aspect of their online presence is a key element in understanding the manipulative dynamic. The public image served as a smokescreen, obscuring the underlying tension and control. Laundrie effectively used social media as a tool to further his manipulation, presenting a facade of normality that masked the disturbing reality of their relationship. This is a crucial aspect of understanding the psychology of control – the ability to curate a public persona that contradicts the private reality. The jarring disconnect between the seemingly perfect Instagram posts and the escalating domestic disputes further underscores the insidious nature of his manipulation.

Laundrie's control extended beyond subtle verbal manipulation. He exerted significant control over their finances, a common tactic in abusive relationships. By controlling the flow of money, he subtly limited Petito's independence, creating a dependence that further cemented his power. This financial control isn't always overtly coercive; it can manifest as subtle decisions about shared funds, limiting Petito's access to money, or controlling joint accounts. The lack of complete financial independence can leave a victim vulnerable and trapped, making it more challenging to leave the relationship. Financial control, when coupled with other forms of manipulation, creates a powerful web of dependence that binds the victim to the abuser.

The manipulation also manifested in the context of their travel plans and itinerary. While appearing collaborative on the surface, Laundrie exerted control over their movements and daily activities, limiting Petito's freedom and opportunities for independent action. This control wasn't always explicitly stated; it often manifested as subtle suggestions or veiled directives, making it more challenging for Petito to resist. The changing of plans without consultation, the seemingly arbitrary decisions about where they'd go and what they'd do, all contributed to a subtle erosion of Petito's autonomy. These seemingly minor decisions, accumulated over time, created a pervasive sense of dependence and limited her ability to make independent choices. This control over movement and routine is a hallmark of controlling behavior, limiting the victim's access to support networks and independent decision-making.

Furthermore, the lack of communication between Petito and her family during certain periods of their trip raises serious concerns about Laundrie's manipulative tactics. The abrupt cessation of communication, coupled with the carefully crafted social media posts, created a false sense of security for Petito's family, delaying their efforts to intervene and check on her well-being. This calculated manipulation of information served to further isolate Petito and obstruct any external intervention.

The specific instances of Laundrie's manipulative behavior, while difficult to definitively document with absolute certainty due to the absence of direct testimony from Petito, can be inferred from a combination of sources. The available evidence, including police reports, witness accounts, and recovered texts, paints a disturbing picture of a controlling, manipulative relationship. While we can't definitively reconstruct every instance of manipulation, the patterns are clear and consistent with known behaviors of abusers. The sheer volume of seemingly innocuous actions, all pointing toward a consistent pattern of control, paints a troubling portrait.

The impact of this gaslighting and manipulation on Gabby Petito is undeniable. The erosion of her self-esteem, the loss of autonomy, and the isolation from her support network created a vulnerability that ultimately contributed to her tragic demise. Understanding the dynamics of gaslighting is crucial not only to comprehend the circumstances surrounding her death but also to recognize and prevent similar tragedies in the future. The case serves as a stark warning about the insidious nature of psychological abuse, highlighting the importance of recognizing the subtle signs and taking proactive steps to intervene. The aftermath of her death has spurred increased awareness of domestic violence, its insidious forms, and the vital role of intervention and support. The case of Gabby Petito and Brian Laundrie stands as a chilling example of how psychological manipulation can have devastating and fatal consequences. Their story underscores the urgency of educating ourselves and others about these dynamics and the need to create a safer environment for victims of abuse. The lingering questions surrounding the precise details of the final days remain, but the broader picture of manipulative control is undeniably clear. The tragic narrative serves as a cautionary tale, a stark reminder of the pervasive and deadly power of psychological abuse.

The Impact on Gabby Psychological Trauma and Resilience

The chilling narrative of Gabby Petito's life and death underscores a terrifying truth: the insidious nature of psychological abuse can be far more devastating than physical violence. While the physical aspects of her final moments remain shrouded in some mystery, the psychological trauma inflicted upon her by Brian Laundrie is undeniable. Understanding the impact of this abuse on Gabby is crucial not only to comprehend the tragedy but also to shed light on the resilience demonstrated by victims in such situations.

Gabby, judging from her social media presence and accounts from friends and family, presented herself as a vibrant, adventurous young woman with a zest for life. Her meticulously curated Instagram feed, filled with breathtaking landscapes and seemingly joyful moments, showcased a carefully constructed image – an image that masked a darker reality. The contrast between this public persona and the underlying turmoil highlights the deceptive nature of domestic abuse. The carefully crafted narrative of a happy couple traveling the country stands in stark contrast to the escalating tension and manipulative control that characterized their relationship behind closed doors.

The psychological impact of Laundrie's manipulation began subtly, with seemingly innocuous comments and actions that gradually eroded Gabby's self-esteem. This is a common tactic in abusive relationships – a slow, insidious process of undermining the victim's confidence and sense of self-worth. Gaslighting, as this tactic is known, involves distorting reality, making the victim question their own sanity and perceptions. This constant subtle undermining of her reality is confirmed through an analysis of her communications. Texts exchanged between Gabby and her family reveal a growing dependence on Brian's approval, and an increasing anxiety over even minor disagreements. The tone shifts from the confident, independent young woman showcased in early texts to someone increasingly uncertain and seeking reassurance.

The seemingly minor disagreements, documented in the recovered texts and calls, often involved conflicts over their travel plans, expenses, and even seemingly trivial daily decisions. What is most alarming is not the disagreements themselves, but the pattern they reveal. Brian systematically, through subtle and seemingly insignificant remarks, turned these disagreements into battles in which Gabby increasingly felt she was in the wrong. This is classic emotional manipulation. He didn't physically restrain or threaten her, but rather, he controlled the narrative, subtly shifting the blame and making Gabby doubt her own perception of events. The cumulative effect of these small, constant attacks on her self-worth was devastating.

The constant stress and anxiety generated by this manipulative behavior manifested in various ways. Reports from witnesses who encountered the couple noted increasing tension and arguments, even in public settings. These incidents, while perhaps not overtly violent, indicate the pervasive and constant pressure Gabby was under. The very act of constantly monitoring her behaviour and responses, of carefully controlling the narrative, is a form of emotional abuse that takes a heavy toll on the victim's mental well-being.

The financial control exerted by Brian further limited Gabby's ability to escape the toxic dynamic. While the exact details of their joint finances remain partially unclear, the available evidence suggests he managed most of their finances, potentially leaving Gabby financially dependent on him. This is another typical tactic employed by abusers, to limit the victim's independence and freedom to leave the relationship. The lack of financial autonomy added to the feeling of helplessness and entrapment. The psychological impact of this financial control is to increase the victim's dependence, deepening the cycle of abuse.

Beyond the financial control, Brian also exerted control over their travel plans and daily activities. This subtle manipulation of their itinerary, seemingly arbitrary decisions that often limited Gabby's ability to connect with loved ones or engage in activities independent of Brian, further isolated her and restricted her access to support. While he presented their trip as a collaborative adventure, his actions demonstrate a systematic effort to control her movement and limit her autonomy. This is a common tactic of abusers, as it isolates the victim from external support and increases their dependence on the abuser.

The eventual silence from Gabby to her family is particularly troubling. This wasn't a simple case of poor cell service or lack of opportunity to communicate. The abrupt cessation of communication, coupled with the carefully maintained public image on social media, points to a deliberate effort by Brian to isolate Gabby from her support system and prevent external intervention. This calculated manipulation of information, the deliberate withholding of communication, added another layer to the psychological abuse. The lack of contact only amplified the family's growing concern, leading to the frantic efforts to find her which were unfortunately too late.

However, amidst the horror, Gabby's story also reveals remarkable resilience. The available evidence suggests she attempted, albeit unsuccessfully, to reach out for help, indicating her determination to break free. Despite the insidious and pervasive nature of Laundrie's manipulative tactics, Gabby's efforts to communicate with her family and friends demonstrate a courage and desire to escape the toxic situation. Her reaching out, even in the face of immense pressure, showcases her strength and resistance to the control Laundrie exerted. Although her attempts to escape were ultimately unsuccessful, the very act of trying speaks volumes about her inner strength and unwillingness to passively accept her situation.

The tragedy of Gabby's death should not obscure the profound psychological impact of the abuse she endured. Her story highlights the insidious nature of domestic violence and the importance of recognizing the subtle signs. It also serves as a testament to the strength and resilience of victims and the vital need for support systems and intervention strategies. While Gabby's experience ended in heartbreak, her story serves as a critical reminder of the need to recognize, understand, and address the pervasive issue of domestic violence and psychological manipulation. The impact on survivors extends far beyond the immediate event, leaving lasting scars on their mental and emotional well-being. Understanding the complex interplay of trauma, resilience, and recovery is essential to provide appropriate support and aid to those who have experienced similar situations. The aftermath of Gabby's death has fostered increased awareness, leading to vital conversations about domestic violence prevention, support systems, and policy changes aimed at protecting vulnerable individuals. While the loss remains profound, her story has also become a catalyst for positive change, prompting important discussions and concrete actions to combat domestic violence and protect future victims. This broader impact of her story should not be overlooked. It is a testament to her legacy and the strength of the individuals who have sought to honor her memory by improving safety and support for victims of abuse.

Seeking Help Resources and Support for Victims

The chilling reality of Gabby Petito's story underscores the urgent need to address the pervasive issue of domestic violence and the crucial role of support systems in helping victims escape abusive relationships. While Gabby's tragic end serves as a stark warning, it also highlights the strength and resilience demonstrated by those who bravely seek help. Breaking the cycle of abuse is a complex process, but it is undeniably possible, and the availability of resources and support is vital to making that possibility a reality for survivors.

It is essential to understand that seeking help is not a sign of weakness, but rather a courageous act of self-preservation. Victims of domestic violence often grapple with feelings of shame, guilt, and fear, making it difficult to reach out for assistance. Abusers often isolate their victims, fostering a sense of dependence and preventing them from seeking external support. The manipulative tactics employed by abusers can make victims question their own perceptions of reality, reinforcing their isolation and hindering their ability to seek help. This insidious control, as evidenced in Gabby's case, is a significant barrier to escape.

However, numerous organizations are dedicated to providing comprehensive support to victims of domestic violence, offering a lifeline to those who are struggling. These resources range from immediate crisis intervention to long-term therapeutic support, addressing the multifaceted needs of survivors. Understanding the range of services available is the first step in empowering victims to take control of their lives and break free from the cycle of abuse.

One of the most crucial resources is the National Domestic Violence Hotline. This hotline operates 24/7, providing confidential support and guidance to victims and those who are concerned about someone they know. Trained advocates are available to listen without judgment, offer immediate crisis intervention, and provide information on local resources such as shelters, legal assistance, and therapy. The hotline's anonymity and accessibility make it a vital lifeline for individuals who may be hesitant to seek help through other channels. The ease of access and the trained professionals make it a crucial resource that can bridge the gap between fear and action.

Beyond the hotline, a vast network of local and national organizations offer specialized services for victims of domestic violence. These organizations often operate shelters that provide safe housing, food, and essential support services for survivors and their children. Shelters offer a safe haven, allowing victims to escape immediate danger and begin the process of healing and rebuilding their lives. They provide a confidential environment where individuals can receive emotional support, access legal and social services, and develop a personalized safety plan. The importance of physical safety cannot be overstated when considering the initial steps to escape an abusive relationship.

In addition to shelter, many organizations offer legal assistance to victims of domestic violence. This support is essential for securing restraining orders, navigating legal proceedings, and obtaining custody of children. Legal advocates play an invaluable role in helping survivors understand their rights, navigate the complexities of the legal system, and secure protection from their abusers. Understanding the legal pathways and having a knowledgeable advocate by their side can greatly increase a victim's ability to establish a safe and independent future.

Therapeutic services play a critical role in the healing process for survivors of domestic violence. Therapy provides a safe and confidential space for victims to process their trauma, address underlying emotional issues, and develop coping mechanisms to manage the long-term psychological effects of abuse. Individual and group therapy can be immensely beneficial in helping survivors to understand their experiences, reclaim their self-worth, and build a stronger sense of self. This form of support tackles the deep psychological damage caused by emotional abuse, and often leads to significantly better outcomes long-term for victims.

The internet also provides a wealth of information and resources for victims of domestic violence. Websites such as the National Coalition Against Domestic Violence (NCADV) offer comprehensive information on domestic violence, including its definition, signs, and effects. These sites offer practical guidance on safety planning, legal options, and accessing support services. The readily available information allows individuals to educate themselves on the issues and resources available at a moment when immediate access is often needed.

It's crucial to remember that the process of escaping an abusive relationship and rebuilding one's life is not a linear one. It's a journey that requires patience, resilience, and consistent support. Setbacks are common, and it is vital for survivors to acknowledge and address these challenges. Continued support from therapists, support groups, and loved ones is often needed to navigate the complexities of recovery and prevent relapse into abusive patterns.

Furthermore, the support system should extend to include friends, family, and community members. Educating others about the signs of domestic violence and encouraging them to offer support to those in need can create a safety net for victims. A supportive community reduces the isolation often felt by victims, providing emotional strength and practical assistance as they navigate the difficult process of escaping an abusive situation.

Gabby Petito's story, while undeniably tragic, underscores the critical need for readily available and accessible resources for victims of domestic violence. The resources and support systems outlined above are crucial in empowering survivors to break free from the cycle of abuse, heal from their trauma, and rebuild their lives. Seeking help is not a sign of weakness; it is an act of courage and self-preservation, and the availability of support is vital in ensuring that victims have the opportunity to thrive beyond their experiences. The fight against domestic violence requires a multifaceted approach, encompassing prevention, intervention and support.

Understanding the psychology of control and manipulation, as highlighted in Gabby's case, is crucial to recognizing the subtle signs of abuse and intervening effectively. The emphasis on proactive education and increased awareness within communities, coupled with readily available and accessible resources, is vital in preventing future tragedies and empowering survivors to seek and receive the help they need and deserve.

The path to healing is rarely straightforward, and setbacks are inevitable. However, with the right support and unwavering dedication to self-care, survivors can rebuild their lives and find a path towards wholeness and empowerment. The journey of healing involves reclaiming agency, establishing independence, and fostering emotional well-being. Through consistent access to resources and the strength of their own resilience, survivors can transcend the trauma of their past and create a future filled with hope, safety, and lasting well-being. The enduring legacy of Gabby Petito's story should be not just the horror of her death, but the increased awareness and resources devoted to preventing such tragedies in the future. Her memory serves as a constant reminder of the importance of intervening, supporting, and empowering those caught in the cycle of domestic violence.

Chapter Five

The Internet's True Crime Obsession

The Gabby Petito Case A Social Media Phenomenon

The Gabby Petito case transcended the confines of a typical missing person investigation, rapidly evolving into a full-blown social media phenomenon that captivated millions worldwide. Its explosive spread across various digital platforms—from TikTok and Instagram to Facebook and Twitter—underscored the increasingly intertwined relationship between true crime, social media, and public discourse. The sheer volume of content generated, from amateur sleuthing to impassioned debates, demonstrated the power of online communities to shape narratives and influence investigations.

The immediacy and accessibility of social media played a critical role in disseminating information about Gabby's disappearance. Unlike previous cases, where information trickled out slowly through traditional media outlets, news of Gabby's vanishing spread like wildfire across countless timelines and feeds. Users shared photos, videos, and snippets of information, creating a constantly updating, albeit often chaotic, picture of the unfolding events. This real-time, crowd-sourced coverage fostered a sense of collective involvement, blurring the lines between passive spectators and active participants.

Instagram, with its visual focus, became a key platform for disseminating details of Gabby's case. Her meticulously curated, idyllic travel photos, posted just weeks before her disappearance, created a stark contrast with the chilling reality of her fate. This juxtaposition fueled public fascination, raising questions about the hidden tensions within what appeared to be a picture-perfect relationship. The platform's algorithm amplified these posts, making the story visible to a vast audience, well beyond Gabby's immediate circle of friends and family.

TikTok, known for its short-form video content, also became a significant player in the Gabby Petito story. Users created countless videos analyzing evidence, speculating on the timeline of events, and offering their own interpretations of the case. The platform's ease of use and its capacity for viral spread allowed for rapid dissemination of information, both accurate and inaccurate, contributing to the case's widespread attention. The speed at which information could be shared on TikTok made it an ideal environment for both disseminating credible information and the spread of conspiracy theories and misinformation, highlighting both the positive and negative potential of the platform.

Facebook and Twitter, established social media platforms, provided avenues for more in-depth discussions, analysis, and the sharing of official updates from law enforcement agencies. While these platforms often hosted more nuanced conversations, they also became battlegrounds for competing narratives and heated debates. The constant flow of information, often conflicting and unverified, added to the intensity of public engagement and highlighted the challenges of separating truth from conjecture in the digital realm.

The appeal of the Gabby Petito case extends beyond its tragic nature. Several factors contributed to its extraordinary resonance with millions: the seemingly idyllic couple's road trip, the contrast between the social media persona and the grim reality, and the relatable aspects of a young couple's journey gone awry. The case tapped into a collective anxiety surrounding relationships, the dangers of domestic violence, and the potential for seemingly perfect lives to mask underlying dysfunction. The story struck a chord with those who could relate to the joys and frustrations of travel, the complexities of romantic relationships, and the pervasiveness of social media's influence on our perception of reality.

The widespread dissemination of Gabby's meticulously documented Instagram journey fueled public engagement. Images of breathtaking landscapes juxtaposed with seemingly happy couple photos created a powerful narrative tension. Viewers were drawn into a curated world that concealed a dark undercurrent of escalating conflict. The contrast between the carefully constructed online image and the heartbreaking reality fueled public fascination and propelled the case into the global spotlight.

The "van life" aesthetic, popularized by social media influencers, added another layer of intrigue. Gabby and Brian's journey resonated with a demographic drawn to the freedom and adventure associated with van life, highlighting the appeal and allure of such a lifestyle, while also underscoring the hidden perils and challenges that can accompany it. This added a sense of vicarious participation for many viewers, further intensifying their engagement with the unfolding tragedy.

The case also tapped into a deep-seated fascination with true crime. True crime narratives, whether in podcasts, documentaries, or books, have experienced a surge in popularity in recent years. Gabby's story, with its elements of mystery, romance, and violence, fit perfectly into this established genre, attracting an already sizable and engaged audience. The social media platforms provided a readily accessible space for this audience to share their thoughts, theories, and emotions, transforming the case into a collective, participatory experience.

The online sleuthing that characterized the Gabby Petito case is a significant aspect of this social media phenomenon. Users meticulously combed through social media posts, videos, and other available information to piece together the timeline of events, forming their own hypotheses about what happened. While some of this online detective work proved helpful to investigators, much of it consisted of speculation and the spread of misinformation, demonstrating both the constructive and destructive potential of this form of crowd-sourced investigation.

The level of online engagement also presented challenges to law enforcement. The constant flow of information, some of it inaccurate or misleading, created challenges in managing the narrative and disseminating reliable information to the public. Social media, while proving a valuable tool in raising awareness and mobilizing support, also created a complex communication environment that required careful navigation. The pressure of public scrutiny and the potential for online misinformation to affect the investigation presented novel challenges for law enforcement agencies in the digital age.

The Gabby Petito case served as a stark reminder of the double-edged sword of social media. While it amplified awareness of domestic violence and helped mobilize support for Gabby's family, it also highlighted the dangers of online misinformation, the potential for sensationalism, and the complexities of navigating public discourse in the digital age. The case underscores the importance of critical media consumption, the need for reliable sources of information, and the role of social media in shaping public perception and influencing investigations. The case's impact extends beyond its tragic narrative, serving as a case study in the evolving intersection of true crime, social media, and public discourse. The rapid spread of information, both accurate and inaccurate, the fervent online speculation, and the unprecedented level of public engagement demonstrated the profound influence of social media in shaping our understanding of events and influencing the course of justice. The case's enduring legacy is a complex one, highlighting the need for responsible online participation and mindful media consumption in the digital age.

True Crime Culture Consumption and Commodification

The Gabby Petito case, while undeniably tragic, became something more: a cultural touchstone. Its rapid dissemination across various digital platforms wasn't simply a reflection of the 24/7 news cycle; it signified a deeper societal fascination with true crime, a hunger amplified and distorted by the unique characteristics of the internet. This wasn't merely about following a breaking news story; it was a participatory spectacle, a collective descent into the details of a young woman's disappearance and death, played out in real-time across millions of screens.

The sheer volume of content generated around the case – from amateur sleuths dissecting blurry screenshots to influencers weaving narratives around the seemingly idyllic Instagram aesthetic– points to a profound shift in how we consume tragedy. The internet, with its insatiable appetite for content, transformed a personal loss into a shared experience, a public performance of grief and speculation. This transformation, however, raises complex ethical questions about the boundaries of empathy, the commodification of suffering, and the potential for exploitation of victims and their families.

The motivations behind this obsession are multifaceted. Some viewers are drawn to the inherent mystery, the puzzle-solving aspect of piecing together fragmented information to arrive at some semblance of understanding. Others are captivated by the dramatic narrative arc, the unfolding drama played out daily on their newsfeeds. For some, it's a morbid curiosity, a voyeuristic glimpse into the dark underbelly of human nature. And for many, the case resonated on a deeply personal level, tapping into anxieties about relationships, travel, and the often-deceptive nature of social media.

The readily available nature of information, however, also contributed significantly to the intensity of the engagement. Unlike past cases that were initially confined to the local news cycle, the details of Gabby's story instantly reached a global audience. This immediate access fueled the constant speculation, often leading to a frenzied race to offer interpretations, whether informed or uninformed. This immediacy often created a sense of urgency and participation, blending the lines between observation and involvement in a way that traditional media couldn't replicate. The constant barrage of updates, theories, and counter-theories produced an environment where factual information frequently collided with rumor and conjecture.

The commodification of the Gabby Petito case is equally striking. News outlets, podcasts, and documentary filmmakers rapidly capitalized on the public's interest, producing a flood of content aiming to tap into the widespread fascination. While some of this content provided legitimate coverage and analysis, much of it veered into sensationalism, exploiting the tragedy for financial gain. The proliferation of clickbait headlines and manipulative thumbnails, designed to maximize engagement, exemplifies the ethical challenges of monetizing real-life suffering.

Moreover, the commercialization of the case extended beyond media outlets. Merchandise bearing Gabby's image, or imagery associated with the case, quickly appeared online. This ranged from t-shirts and mugs to stickers and phone cases, transforming a deeply personal loss into a profit-generating opportunity. Such blatant commercialization further underscores the moral ambiguities surrounding the commodification of grief and the ethics of profiting from tragedy The question remains: at what point does the pursuit of public interest cross into exploitation?

The impact of this obsession on Gabby's family deserves careful consideration. The intense public interest, while initially offering a sense of support and widespread awareness, also brought significant burdens. The family was subjected to relentless media scrutiny, their privacy invaded by an insatiable public thirst for information.

The constant barrage of news coverage, online speculation, and intrusive media attention only added to their profound grief and loss. The impact on the emotional well-being of the family cannot be overstated; the constant exposure to a morbidly curious public created an additional layer of trauma and hardship. Their experience underscores the crucial need for sensitivity and respect in the face of such public tragedies. It is a stark reminder that the narrative surrounding the case should not overshadow the profound human suffering experienced by those directly affected.

Furthermore, the intense focus on the Gabby Petito case often overshadows similar tragedies. While the case raised awareness about domestic violence and the dangers of controlling relationships, it also risked creating a hierarchy of victimhood. Other missing persons cases, perhaps lacking the same visual appeal or viral potential, received far less attention, raising questions about the biases inherent in our culture of true crime consumption. This selective focus raises important questions about how we prioritize narratives and the potential to disregard other victims who did not have the same level of public support and media coverage.

The ethical implications of this true crime obsession are significant and demand critical examination. While the public's fascination with true crime narratives is understandable, the ease with which these narratives can be manipulated and commodified online is cause for serious concern. The potential for sensationalism, the exploitation of victims' families, and the creation of a culture that prioritizes spectacle over substance all necessitate a broader conversation about ethical media consumption and responsible online participation. We need to develop a more nuanced approach to engaging with true crime narratives, one that prioritizes empathy and respect for those affected, while critically examining the motivations and consequences of our fascination. The Gabby Petito case, therefore, serves as a cautionary tale, underscoring the need for greater awareness and responsibility in how we consume and interact with these often-exploitative forms of popular culture.

The lasting impact of the Gabby Petito case is complex and multifaceted. While it undoubtedly increased public awareness of domestic violence, it also highlighted the darker aspects of online culture, where speculation, misinformation, and the commodification of tragedy are rampant. The case provides a compelling case study for exploring the intersection of true crime, social media, and the challenges of navigating public discourse in the digital age. The intense scrutiny, fueled by 24/7 news coverage and real-time social media updates, created an environment that, while bringing the case to a global audience, also blurred the lines between justice, empathy and exploitation.

Ultimately, the Gabby Petito case serves as a crucial reminder of the need for critical media literacy and mindful online engagement. While true crime narratives can be informative and raise awareness, we must remain vigilant against the pitfalls of sensationalism, the exploitation of victims, and the erosion of ethical boundaries in the pursuit of clickbait and profit. The ongoing conversation surrounding this case should not only center on the tragic circumstances of Gabby's death but also on the broader cultural trends and ethical considerations that it has brought to light, prompting a reflective analysis of our collective obsession with true crime and its impact on society. The enduring challenge is to find a balance between the public's right to know and the need to treat victims and their families with the utmost respect and sensitivity, ensuring that the pursuit of justice is not overshadowed by the spectacle of online attention.

The Ethics of Online Speculation The Role of Citizen Detectives

The Gabby Petito case snowcased, in stark relief, the burgeoning phenomenon of the online citizen detective. Fueled by readily available information and the addictive nature of social media, a vast, largely untrained army of internet users poured over every scrap of digital evidence, constructing their own narratives, theories, and even pronouncements of guilt or innocence. While some contributions proved genuinely helpful to law enforcement, many others introduced significant challenges, highlighting the ethical quagmire inherent in this new form of investigative participation.

The initial outpouring of online sleuthing was understandable. The fragmented nature of the information released by authorities, coupled with the constant stream of updates on social media, created a vacuum that amateur investigators felt compelled to fill. Individuals, driven by a mixture of empathy, curiosity, and perhaps a touch of self-importance, dove into the digital debris, combing through Gabby and Brian's social media posts, analyzing their geolocation data, and scrutinizing even the most inconsequential details for clues. This online detective work, often driven by a desire for justice and a need to make sense of a senseless tragedy, created a sense of collective engagement that transcended geographical boundaries. The shared pursuit of truth, fueled by a rapidly evolving digital tapestry of evidence, transformed the case into a global, online collaborative effort.

However, the inherent limitations and potential dangers of this citizen detective movement quickly became apparent. The lack of formal training and experience among these digital sleuths led to numerous misinterpretations and the proliferation of misinformation. The blurry images, incomplete data, and ambiguous social media posts were often subjected to speculation that stretched the boundaries of reality, transforming assumptions into "facts" and conjecture into concrete evidence. The very tools meant to facilitate information sharing – social media platforms –often became breeding grounds for unsubstantiated accusations and harmful narratives. The speed at which information (and misinformation) traveled dwarfed the capacity for careful verification, leading to a situation where unfounded claims gained traction with alarming speed.

The spread of false information significantly impacted the case and those involved. Misleading interpretations of Brian Laundrie's movements, or Gabby's last online interactions, fueled speculation that often deviated from the actual investigative leads. These unfounded claims not only consumed valuable investigative time, but also created a climate of uncertainty and suspicion that hampered the official investigation. They also had profound implications for the families involved, who were subjected to a relentless barrage of online speculation, much of it unwarranted and deeply hurtful.

One critical aspect of the ethical dilemma relates to the potential for harassment and doxxing. In their zeal to solve the case, some amateur detectives crossed the line from responsible investigation into outright harassment. Individuals who were perceived as being connected to the case, whether directly or indirectly, were subjected to relentless online attacks, their privacy violated, and their lives disrupted. This behavior, often driven by a misguided sense of justice, exposed the dark side of online participation. The ease with which personal information can be accessed and shared online, coupled with the anonymity offered by many platforms, fueled a culture of impunity, where individuals felt empowered to engage in potentially harmful and illegal behavior without consequence.

Moreover, the online pursuit of justice often conflicted with the due process rights of the accused. Brian Laundrie, before his death, became the target of a frenzied online campaign, where accusations of guilt were leveled without the benefit of a fair trial or legal process. This pre-judgment, fueled by online speculation, created a climate of hostility and undermined the principles of justice. The intense public scrutiny, fueled by amateur detectives, created an environment where the presumption of innocence was frequently disregarded, replacing it with a pervasive climate of online condemnation. This created a significant ethical challenge, raising serious questions about the boundaries of online engagement and the potential impact on the legal system.

Furthermore, the online obsession with the case frequently overshadowed other missing persons cases, illustrating a troubling disparity in the allocation of public attention and resources. While Gabby's case captured global attention due to its highly visual and seemingly idyllic initial narrative, countless other missing persons cases received far less media coverage and online scrutiny. This discrepancy highlighted the inherent biases of online engagement, which often favors cases that fit a particular narrative or possess a certain degree of visual appeal. This disparity in attention underscores the need for a more equitable distribution of resources and public concern in addressing missing persons cases, irrespective of their media visibility.

Finally, the commercialization of the case added another layer of ethical complexity. Many individuals and organizations exploited the public interest for profit, creating and selling merchandise, podcasts, and documentaries focused on Gabby's story. While some of these ventures contributed to a broader awareness of domestic violence, many were clearly exploitative, capitalizing on the suffering of a family and the tragedy of a young woman's life. This commercialization of grief raised important questions about the ethical boundaries of profit-making in the context of true crime and the need for a greater sense of responsibility among those who choose to profit from public tragedies.

The emergence of the online citizen detective is a double-edged sword. While the potential for positive contributions to investigations exists, the ethical pitfalls are undeniable. A greater emphasis on media literacy, critical thinking, and a deeper understanding of the legal and social implications of online actions are essential to mitigate the risks associated with this phenomenon. The future of online investigative participation hinges on a commitment to responsible engagement, a respect for the legal process, and a profound awareness of the potential harm that can be inflicted in the pursuit of truth. Only through such a commitment can the benefits of citizen involvement be realized without sacrificing the ethical principles that underpin a just and equitable society. The legacy of the Gabby Petito case, therefore, should serve as a cautionary tale, reminding us of the urgent need for a more responsible and ethical approach to online crime-solving.

The Impact on Law Enforcement Public Pressure and Transparency

The intense public interest in the Gabby Petito case placed unprecedented pressure on law enforcement agencies involved in the investigation. The relentless 24/7 news cycle, fueled by social media's insatiable appetite for updates, created a demanding environment where every action, or inaction, was scrutinized under a microscope. Law enforcement agencies faced a delicate balancing act: maintaining the integrity of the investigation while simultaneously managing the public's insatiable thirst for information. This tension highlighted the profound challenges of conducting a high-profile investigation in the age of instant communication and pervasive online scrutiny.

The initial information released by authorities, often fragmented and deliberately cautious to avoid compromising the investigation, only served to amplify the public's anxieties. This perceived lack of transparency, in the face of the constant stream of online speculation and amateur detective work, fueled a sense of frustration and distrust. The public's expectation of immediate answers, fueled by the readily available information online, clashed with the methodical and often time-consuming nature of a complex criminal investigation. This inherent tension between the need for speed and the demands of a thorough investigation created a significant challenge for law enforcement.

The pressure to provide updates, while simultaneously protecting the integrity of the investigation, created a difficult ethical dilemma. Releasing too much information risked compromising investigative leads and potentially jeopardizing the prosecution of any potential suspects. However, withholding information only served to fuel speculation and further erode public trust. This precarious balance required a level of strategic communication and public relations expertise rarely seen in previous investigations. Law enforcement agencies were forced to navigate a complex landscape, often making difficult choices between protecting the investigation and managing public expectations.

The case also highlighted the limitations of traditional law enforcement communication strategies in the digital age. The speed and reach of social media far surpassed the ability of law enforcement agencies to control the narrative. Misinformation spread like wildfire, fueled by unreliable sources and the inherent biases of online platforms. This uncontrolled information flow often overshadowed official statements and updates, creating a challenging information environment that hampered the investigation and eroded public trust. The need for more agile and responsive communication strategies, capable of adapting to the rapid pace of online dissemination, became apparent.

Furthermore, the case revealed the vulnerability of law enforcement agencies to online harassment and cyberbullying. Officers involved in the investigation, as well as those perceived as having mishandled aspects of the case, became targets of online attacks. Their personal information was often shared without their consent, exposing them and their families to significant risks. This demonstrated a disturbing lack of accountability for online behavior and the potentially devastating consequences of digital aggression. The need for better protection and support for law enforcement officers facing online harassment became evident.

The intense public scrutiny also raised concerns about the potential for undue influence on the investigative process. The pressure to solve the case quickly and satisfy public expectations could potentially compromise the objectivity and thoroughness of the investigation. The fear of public backlash or criticism could lead to shortcuts or compromises in investigative procedures, undermining the integrity of the judicial process. Maintaining impartiality in the face of intense public pressure emerged as a critical challenge for law enforcement.

The Gabby Petito case served as a stark reminder of the inherent complexities of balancing public transparency with the need to protect the integrity of a criminal investigation. The constant pressure to satisfy public demands for immediate answers, in conjunction with the rapid spread of misinformation online, created significant challenges for law enforcement. The case underscored the urgent need for improved communication strategies, enhanced protections for law enforcement officers from online harassment, and a more nuanced understanding of the ethical and practical challenges of conducting high-profile investigations in the digital age. The lessons learned from this case are critical for shaping future responses to similar situations, ensuring that public interest is balanced with the requirements of a fair and impartial investigation.

Beyond the immediate challenges, the case also prompted a wider discussion about the role of social media in criminal investigations. The widespread sharing of potentially sensitive information, including crime scene photos and personal details of those involved, raised serious ethical and legal concerns. The lack of regulation and oversight on online platforms allowed misinformation to proliferate, while the anonymity afforded by many platforms emboldened online harassment and the spread of unsubstantiated claims. The case highlighted the need for greater regulation and accountability within social media companies to prevent the misuse of their platforms in criminal investigations.

Moreover, the Gabby Petito case triggered a renewed focus on the importance of domestic violence awareness and prevention. The tragically violent end to Gabby's life served as a jarring wake-up call, emphasizing the pervasive nature of domestic abuse and the urgent need for societal change. While the case itself highlighted the limitations of law enforcement's response to domestic violence calls, it also fostered a broader conversation about improved training, better resource allocation, and the development of more effective strategies for preventing and intervening in domestic violence situations. This increased awareness, while born from tragedy, underscored the powerful impact of high-profile cases in influencing social change.

The legal ramifications of the case extended beyond the immediate investigation into the realm of digital forensics and the admissibility of online evidence in court. The reliance on social media posts, geolocation data, and other digital information raised important questions about the authenticity, reliability, and legal admissibility of such evidence. The increasing prevalence of digital evidence in criminal investigations necessitates a clearer understanding of legal standards regarding its collection, preservation, and use in court proceedings. The complexities of digital forensics, coupled with the ever-evolving nature of digital technology, required a reassessment of existing legal frameworks.

Finally, the long-term impact of the Gabby Petito case on law enforcement practices and public perception is still unfolding. The case prompted a critical examination of existing policies and procedures related to missing persons investigations, domestic violence response, and the management of public information during high-profile cases. It also fostered a renewed discussion about the ethical responsibilities of law enforcement in balancing public transparency with the need to protect the integrity of the investigative process. The legacy of this case will undoubtedly shape the approach of law enforcement agencies to future investigations, emphasizing the need for improved communication strategies, increased transparency, and greater sensitivity to the needs of victims and their families. The enduring impact of this case underlines the lasting consequences of high-profile criminal events on law enforcement practices, legal frameworks, and public perception.

The Future of True Crime and Social Media Navigating the Digital Landscape

The Gabby Petito case, dissected and analyzed across countless online forums and news channels, served as a stark illustration of the power—and the peril—of the internet's true crime obsession. It revealed a digital landscape where speculation often outpaced fact, where amateur sleuths wielded the power of social media to influence investigations, and where the line between responsible reporting and reckless dissemination blurred dangerously. This wasn't simply a case of voyeurism; it represented a fundamental shift in how true crime stories are consumed, investigated, and ultimately, judged. The future of true crime reporting hinges on navigating this complex digital ecosystem responsibly, understanding its potential for both good and immense harm.

One of the most significant challenges lies in the speed at which information, both accurate and inaccurate, spreads online. The immediacy of social media platforms creates an environment where preliminary reports, often incomplete or even misleading, can gain traction before official statements are released. This phenomenon, frequently observed during the Petito investigation, can lead to the propagation of misinformation, hindering the investigative process and potentially damaging the reputations of individuals involved. The spread of unsubstantiated theories, fueled by online echo chambers, not only obstructs justice but can also cause significant distress to the families of victims and suspects alike.

The rise of "citizen journalism" presents another complex layer. While the public's desire to participate in uncovering the truth is understandable, the lack of journalistic training and ethical guidelines among online sleuths can lead to irresponsible reporting. The sharing of potentially sensitive information, including crime scene photos, personal details of witnesses or suspects, and even speculative theories presented as fact, can compromise investigations and infringe on the privacy rights of individuals. The need for responsible digital citizenship, especially in the context of high-profile true crime cases, cannot be overstated.

Moving forward, a crucial step towards responsible online behavior lies in media literacy education. Equipping the public with the skills to critically evaluate online information, identify misinformation, and understand the ethical implications of sharing sensitive content is paramount. This includes promoting media literacy initiatives in schools, libraries, and community centers, as well as creating easily accessible online resources to help individuals navigate the complexities of the digital information landscape.

Furthermore, greater accountability on the part of social media platforms is necessary. While these platforms offer a valuable platform for communication and information sharing, they also bear a responsibility to mitigate the spread of misinformation and harmful content. This could involve implementing stricter policies regarding the sharing of sensitive information related to ongoing investigations, developing more robust mechanisms for identifying and removing false or misleading content, and providing greater support to users in identifying and reporting questionable information.

Law enforcement agencies, too, need to adapt to the digital age. While maintaining the integrity of an investigation is paramount, the public's right to information must also be considered. A more transparent and proactive approach to communication, while carefully safeguarding sensitive details, is necessary. This could involve regular press briefings, utilizing official social media channels to provide updates and dispel misinformation, and actively engaging with the public in a responsible and ethical manner.

The ethical dilemmas extend beyond the dissemination of information. The use of facial recognition technology, geolocation data, and other digital tools in investigations raises significant privacy concerns. Balancing the investigative needs with the protection of individual privacy requires careful consideration of legal and ethical guidelines. Strict regulations and oversight are needed to ensure that these powerful technologies are used responsibly and do not infringe on fundamental human rights.

The role of the media in the digital age is undergoing a profound transformation. Traditional news outlets, grappling with the rapid spread of online content, need to adapt their reporting practices to maintain credibility and responsibility. This includes embracing rigorous fact-checking procedures, providing clear context to stories, and acknowledging the limitations of preliminary information. The competition for online attention shouldn't compromise journalistic integrity; ethical standards must remain paramount.

The Gabby Petito case highlighted the crucial need for collaboration between law enforcement, the media, and the public. By fostering a culture of responsible information sharing and promoting media literacy, we can mitigate the risks associated with the internet's true crime obsession and ensure that investigations are conducted ethically and effectively. The digital age necessitates a new approach to true crime reporting, one that prioritizes responsible behavior and understands the ethical implications of each online action. The future of true crime hinges on this understanding.

Ultimately, the internet's true crime obsession isn't inherently negative. It can fuel public interest in justice, promote discussion about important social issues like domestic violence, and even contribute to solving crimes through the sharing of information. However, this positive potential is only realized through responsible behavior and a commitment to ethical principles. The challenges are significant, requiring a multifaceted approach that addresses the roles and responsibilities of social media platforms, law enforcement agencies, the media, and the public itself. The long-term impact of the internet's influence on true crime narrative will be determined by our collective ability to navigate these complex ethical considerations.

The future of true crime and social media is inextricably linked, a dynamic relationship demanding constant vigilance and adaptation. It requires a thoughtful dialogue, involving all stakeholders, to establish clear guidelines for responsible online behavior, ensuring that the pursuit of justice is not compromised by the uncontrolled spread of misinformation and the potential for undue influence on investigations. The ongoing conversation surrounding ethical reporting, responsible online participation, and the need for stricter regulations on social media platforms is essential for navigating this evolving landscape. The aim should be to harness the power of digital technology to improve justice while simultaneously mitigating its potential to inflict harm. The journey towards a more responsible and ethical digital landscape for true crime narratives is an ongoing process, demanding continual engagement and critical assessment from all parties involved. Only through this collective effort can we hope to prevent future tragedies from being amplified and distorted by the unchecked power of the internet. The responsibility for shaping this future rests not solely on any one entity, but on each individual who participates in the online discourse surrounding true crime.

Chapter Six

Lessons Learned and Lasting Impact

Policy Changes and Advocacy Efforts A Call for Action

The outpouring of grief and outrage following Gabby Petito's death transcended the confines of a single tragedy; it ignited a national conversation about domestic violence, its pervasive nature, and the shortcomings of systems designed to protect victims. The intensity of public reaction, fueled by the relentless coverage and the accessibility of information through social media, created an unprecedented level of pressure on lawmakers and law enforcement agencies to address the systemic issues that allowed Gabby's story to unfold as it did. This pressure translated into tangible policy changes and advocacy efforts across multiple levels of government and within various organizations dedicated to ending domestic violence.

One of the most immediate and significant impacts of the Petito case was the renewed focus on improving law enforcement's response to domestic violence calls. The investigation revealed instances where opportunities to intervene and prevent the tragic outcome may have been missed. While the exact details of the law enforcement response remain a subject of debate, the case underscored the need for more comprehensive training for officers in recognizing the signs of domestic abuse, understanding the dynamics of abusive relationships, and effectively investigating such cases. Many jurisdictions responded by implementing mandatory training programs focusing on lethality assessment, victim-centered approaches, and recognizing the red flags that often precede escalating violence. These programs often include scenario-based training, designed to simulate real-life encounters with victims of domestic violence and perpetrators. The aim is not just to improve investigative techniques, but also to instill empathy and sensitivity among officers handling these complex and sensitive situations.

Beyond training, several states and municipalities re-evaluated their existing domestic violence protocols and enacted legislation aimed at strengthening protective orders and enhancing the ability of victims to seek help. The focus shifted from reactive measures to proactive prevention. This included improving communication between different law enforcement agencies, ensuring seamless information sharing across jurisdictional boundaries, and enhancing data collection to track the effectiveness of interventions. Some states increased funding for domestic violence shelters and support services, while others expanded the eligibility criteria for receiving assistance. Several jurisdictions implemented specialized units focused specifically on domestic violence, aiming to provide a more consistent and coordinated response. The goal was to shift the paradigm from viewing domestic violence as a private matter to recognizing it as a serious crime requiring swift and decisive action.

The Gabby Petito case also highlighted the limitations of relying solely on law enforcement to address the complex issue of domestic violence. Advocacy groups seized the opportunity to promote awareness of the resources available to victims and to educate the public about the warning signs of abusive relationships. The tragic events spurred a surge in donations to domestic violence shelters and support organizations, providing them with the resources needed to expand their services and reach a wider audience. This period saw a renewed focus on preventative education, with programs designed to teach young people about healthy relationships, consent, and recognizing the early warning signs of abuse. Schools, community centers, and online platforms became instrumental in disseminating these educational resources, reaching a much wider audience than traditional methods.

The increased visibility of the case also spurred discussions around the role of technology in domestic violence. The use of social media to document aspects of the relationship, albeit superficially, raised questions about the potential for monitoring and intervention through digital means. While privacy concerns remain paramount, the conversation is shifting towards finding responsible ways to use technology to detect signs of abuse, facilitate intervention, and provide support to those who are trapped in violent relationships.

This discussion includes examining the role of social media companies in moderating content and ensuring that platforms are not used to facilitate abusive behavior or spread misinformation that might endanger victims. Some organizations have explored developing technology-based tools that can anonymously detect potentially abusive language or patterns of behavior, thus enabling intervention.

Furthermore, the Gabby Petito case ignited discussions about the broader issue of missing persons investigations. The disparity in the media coverage and investigative resources allocated to Gabby's case, compared to those often afforded to missing persons from marginalized communities, brought to light systemic inequities within law enforcement. This highlighted the urgent need for more equitable and efficient protocols in handling missing persons reports, irrespective of race, ethnicity, or socioeconomic status. The case has prompted many law enforcement agencies to review their missing persons procedures, ensuring a standardized approach to investigations and resource allocation, regardless of the victim's background.

The legislative and policy changes stemming from the Gabby Petito case represent a significant step towards improving the response to domestic violence and protecting victims. However, the fight is far from over. The ongoing challenge lies in ensuring that these changes translate into tangible improvements in the lives of those affected by domestic abuse. This requires ongoing monitoring, evaluation, and adaptation of policies and programs to meet the ever-evolving needs of victims and to address the complex dynamics of abusive relationships. The legacy of Gabby Petito's death should not just be remembered as a tragedy, but as a catalyst for meaningful change, a turning point in how society addresses domestic violence and protects vulnerable individuals.

The path forward necessitates continuous advocacy, research, and collaboration between law enforcement, policymakers, advocacy groups, and the public. Sustained efforts are required to maintain the momentum generated by the initial wave of public concern. This includes ensuring adequate funding for support services, continuing to improve law enforcement training, and promoting public awareness campaigns to educate communities about the signs of abuse and the resources available to those who need help. The focus should not only be on reactive responses but also on proactive measures to prevent domestic violence from ever occurring in the first place.

Ultimately, the lessons learned from the Gabby Petito case extend far beyond the immediate circumstances of her death. They underscore the critical need for a holistic and multifaceted approach to combating domestic violence, involving collaborative action from multiple sectors of society. This means fostering a climate of open dialogue, improving data collection and analysis to track progress and identify areas for improvement, and continually challenging societal norms and attitudes that contribute to the perpetuation of domestic violence. Only through such sustained and concerted efforts can we hope to honor Gabby Petito's memory and prevent future tragedies. The long-term success of these efforts depends on sustained commitment and vigilance, ensuring that the lessons learned from this devastating case are not forgotten but serve as a foundation for a safer and more just future for everyone. The work continues, fueled by the memory of a young life lost and the urgent need to prevent others from suffering the same fate. The challenge is significant, but the potential for positive change, born from tragedy, remains a powerful force for good.

The Legacy of Gabby Petito A Symbol of Hope and Healing

The profound sadness surrounding Gabby Petito's death gave rise to something unexpected: a surge of collective empathy and a renewed determination to confront the pervasive issue of domestic violence. While the tragedy itself was undeniably devastating, it served as a stark and unavoidable wake-up call, forcing society to confront the uncomfortable realities of abusive relationships and the systemic failures that often allow them to flourish. Gabby's story, amplified by the relentless news cycle and the pervasive reach of social media, became a potent symbol, a rallying cry for change that resonated far beyond the confines of her individual experience.

The initial shock and outrage morphed into a sustained movement for reform. The sheer volume of public attention, a testament to the power of social media to both spread information and galvanize action, created an unprecedented level of pressure on lawmakers and law enforcement. This pressure was not fleeting; it translated into concrete policy changes and a significant shift in the national conversation surrounding domestic abuse. The legacy of Gabby Petito isn't just about mourning a life lost; it's about the tangible efforts to prevent similar tragedies from occurring in the future.

One of the most significant and immediate impacts was the heightened scrutiny of law enforcement practices. The investigation into Gabby's death, though ultimately successful in finding her body and apprehending Brian Laundrie, highlighted gaps in how domestic violence cases are handled. The critique wasn't necessarily about individual officer incompetence, but about systemic inadequacies in training, protocols, and resource allocation. The perception, fair or not, was that opportunities to intervene, to prevent the escalation of violence, might have been missed. This criticism prompted a wave of reforms across the country.

Many police departments implemented mandatory training programs focused on recognizing the subtle signs of abuse, understanding the dynamics of power and control in abusive relationships, and effectively investigating domestic violence incidents. These programs went beyond the basics, incorporating advanced training on lethality assessment—techniques for identifying situations with a high risk of homicide—and emphasizing victim-centered approaches that prioritize the safety and well-being of those subjected to abuse. The emphasis shifted from a focus solely on apprehending perpetrators to providing comprehensive support and protection for victims. This included training on de-escalation techniques to reduce the likelihood of violence during interactions with abusive partners. The aim was to equip officers with the skills and knowledge necessary to handle these complex situations with both sensitivity and effectiveness.

Beyond training, there was a significant push to improve inter-agency communication and data sharing. In many cases, the investigation revealed breakdowns in communication between different law enforcement agencies, hindering the effectiveness of investigations. This led to initiatives aimed at streamlining the exchange of information across jurisdictional boundaries, fostering better collaboration, and ensuring a more coordinated response. Improved data collection also became a priority, enabling law enforcement agencies to better track the effectiveness of their interventions and identify areas needing further improvement. The data collected wasn't merely for statistical analysis; it was intended to inform policy decisions and resource allocation.

The Gabby Petito case also highlighted the crucial role of advocacy groups and support organizations in the fight against domestic violence. The tragedy spurred a significant surge in donations and volunteer involvement, empowering these organizations to expand their reach and offer a wider range of services to victims. These organizations played a vital role in providing critical resources, shelter, legal assistance, and counseling to individuals and families affected by domestic abuse. They also played a significant part in shaping the public narrative, educating communities about the signs of abuse and the resources available to those seeking help.

The focus expanded to include preventative education, emphasizing the importance of teaching young people about healthy relationships, consent, and the early warning signs of abuse. Schools, community centers, and online platforms became important channels for disseminating this educational material, reaching a broader audience than traditional methods. The aim wasn't simply to react to instances of abuse but to prevent them from happening in the first place. This focus on prevention, combined with increased support for victims, represented a significant paradigm shift in the approach to domestic violence.

Technological advancements and their role in both facilitating and preventing abuse also came under the microscope. The ubiquitous presence of social media in Gabby's life, as documented through her Instagram posts and other online activity, raised important questions about the intersection of technology and domestic violence. This spurred discussions about the potential uses of technology to monitor, detect, and intervene in potentially abusive situations. While privacy concerns were, and remain, paramount, the conversations around ethically responsible uses of technology continued. This included exploring the role of social media companies in content moderation and the development of tools that could anonymously detect potentially abusive language or patterns of behavior online. The goal is to strike a delicate balance between protecting privacy rights and utilizing technology effectively to aid in the prevention and intervention of domestic violence.

Moreover, the disproportionate media attention surrounding Gabby's case, compared to other missing persons cases, particularly those involving individuals from marginalized communities, forced a reckoning with systemic inequities within law enforcement and the media. This highlighted the urgent need for more equitable and efficient protocols for handling missing persons reports, regardless of race, ethnicity, or socioeconomic status. The case became a catalyst for discussions on implicit biases, unequal allocation of resources, and the need for a more equitable approach to missing persons investigations. This aspect of Gabby's legacy highlighted the interconnectedness of social justice issues and domestic violence.

The impact of Gabby Petito's death is undeniably profound and multifaceted. The changes spurred by her story are far-reaching and continue to evolve. The legislative and policy changes represent significant progress, but the work is far from over. The challenge lies in ensuring the sustained implementation and effectiveness of these reforms. This requires continuous monitoring, evaluation, and adaptation of policies and programs to meet the ever-evolving dynamics of domestic abuse. The legacy of Gabby Petito must be not simply a solemn remembrance of a tragedy but a constant reminder of the need for a collective commitment to eradicating domestic violence. The ongoing dialogue, the continuous advocacy, and the relentless pursuit of justice represent the truest tribute to her memory – a world where no one suffers the same fate. The future of the fight against domestic violence is built on the foundation of lessons learned from her tragic story, a foundation demanding vigilance, perseverance, and an unwavering dedication to a safer, more just world for all.

Improving Law Enforcement Response Addressing Systemic Issues

The tragic death of Gabby Petito exposed deep-seated flaws within the system designed to protect victims of domestic violence. While the investigation ultimately led to the recovery of her remains and the apprehension of Brian Laundrie, the journey highlighted critical shortcomings in law enforcement response that demand immediate and sustained reform. The problem wasn't simply a lack of individual officer competence, but rather a systemic failure originating from inadequate training, flawed protocols, and insufficient inter-agency cooperation. This systemic failure allowed a potentially preventable tragedy to unfold.

One glaring area of concern centers around the training provided to law enforcement officers dealing with domestic violence incidents. Many departments rely on cursory, one-time training sessions that fail to equip officers with the necessary tools to effectively assess and respond to the complex dynamics of abusive relationships. This inadequate training often results in a failure to recognize the subtle, yet crucial, indicators of abuse – the controlling behaviors, the subtle threats, the escalating patterns of violence – that can signal impending danger. Instead of comprehensive training that includes nuanced understanding of coercive control, many officers receive superficial instruction, leaving them ill-equipped to differentiate between a typical domestic dispute and a potentially lethal situation.

Effective training must extend beyond basic awareness. Officers need to be trained in advanced lethality assessment techniques, learning to identify high-risk situations with a heightened potential for homicide. This involves understanding the power and control wheel, recognizing the tactics abusers use to maintain dominance, and assessing the specific risk factors present in each individual case. Moreover, training should be ongoing and updated regularly to reflect the evolving nature of domestic abuse and the latest research in the field. Regular refresher courses, incorporating real-world case studies and interactive scenarios, can significantly improve the ability of officers to identify and respond appropriately to dangerous situations. The emphasis must shift from reactive policing to proactive intervention.

Another critical area requiring immediate attention is the development and implementation of standardized protocols for handling domestic violence calls. The inconsistencies in how different agencies approach these calls highlight a lack of uniformity and coordination that compromises the safety of victims. Standardized protocols, developed collaboratively by experts in domestic violence, law enforcement, and victim advocacy, can provide a clear framework for officers to follow. These protocols should outline clear procedures for responding to domestic violence calls, including mandatory steps like conducting thorough interviews with all parties involved, documenting all evidence meticulously, and ensuring the safety and well-being of the victim.

The protocols must also address the critical issue of lethality assessments, mandating that officers conduct a comprehensive risk assessment to determine the potential for future violence. This assessment should consider the severity and frequency of past abuse, the presence of weapons, the abuser's history of violence, and any potential threats made against the victim. The outcome of this assessment should inform the officer's response, ensuring that appropriate measures are taken to protect the victim, such as issuing a restraining order, connecting the victim with support services, or initiating a criminal investigation. The implementation of these protocols needs to be meticulously monitored and regularly reviewed to guarantee efficacy and responsiveness to evolving circumstances.

Beyond improved training and standardized protocols, there is a crucial need for enhanced inter-agency cooperation and information sharing. Too often, investigations are hampered by breakdowns in communication between different law enforcement agencies. In Gabby Petito's case, the lack of seamless information sharing between jurisdictions might have had critical consequences. Implementing improved systems for tracking and disseminating critical information is essential to improve the efficiency and effectiveness of domestic violence investigations.

This improved inter-agency collaboration requires the establishment of centralized databases and information-sharing platforms that can be accessed by all relevant agencies. Such platforms could facilitate the immediate sharing of critical information, such as warrants, restraining orders, and police reports, regardless of jurisdictional boundaries. The creation of joint task forces and cross-training opportunities can also promote greater understanding and collaboration between different agencies. By fostering a culture of collaboration and information sharing, law enforcement can significantly enhance their ability to identify and address domestic violence incidents effectively.

Furthermore, the use of technology can play a significant role in improving law enforcement response to domestic violence. The development and implementation of advanced technological tools can assist officers in conducting thorough investigations and identifying potential risks. This includes utilizing GPS tracking to monitor individuals subject to restraining orders, deploying body cameras to record interactions with victims and perpetrators, and employing data analytics to identify patterns and trends in domestic violence incidents. However, the use of technology must be carefully balanced against the need to protect individuals' privacy rights.

The importance of victim-centered approaches cannot be overstated. Law enforcement agencies must shift away from a perpetrator-focused approach to one that prioritizes the safety and well-being of the victim. This requires training officers to conduct sensitive interviews, to actively listen to victims' concerns, and to provide them with access to the necessary support services. It also requires building trust with victims, ensuring that they feel safe and empowered to report abuse without fear of retaliation or judgment. The goal is to create a supportive environment where victims feel comfortable seeking help and trusting the system to protect them.

Finally, there's a critical need for ongoing evaluation and assessment of law enforcement practices related to domestic violence. Regular audits and independent reviews can help identify areas where improvements are needed and ensure that new training programs and protocols are effective. The evaluation should not only focus on the procedural aspects of law enforcement response but also assess the overall impact on victim safety and perpetrator accountability. This data-driven approach will allow for continuous improvement and adaptation of practices to best meet the complex and evolving challenges of domestic violence.

In conclusion, improving law enforcement response to domestic violence requires a multifaceted approach that addresses systemic issues within training, protocols, and inter-agency cooperation. Implementing advanced lethality assessment techniques, standardized protocols, improved inter-agency communication, victim-centered approaches, and technology, combined with ongoing evaluation and assessment, are critical steps towards preventing future tragedies. The legacy of Gabby Petito demands nothing less than a comprehensive overhaul of the system, transforming it from one that inadvertently allows violence to flourish into one that actively protects victims and holds perpetrators accountable. Only then will her tragic death serve as a catalyst for meaningful and lasting change, a testament to a society committed to preventing future tragedies of similar nature.

The Power of Awareness Educating and Empowering Communities

The tragedy of Gabby Petito's death served as a stark reminder of the pervasive nature of domestic violence and the urgent need for societal change. While improving law enforcement response is critical, equally vital is a comprehensive strategy focused on educating and empowering communities to recognize, prevent, and respond to domestic violence. This requires a multi-pronged approach that tackles the issue from several angles, targeting individuals, families, and the broader community.

The first step is education—a fundamental shift in how we understand and address domestic violence. This begins with dispelling pervasive myths and misconceptions. Many still believe domestic violence is a private matter, confined to isolated incidents within dysfunctional families. This misconception allows abuse to fester in silence, often escalating to devastating consequences. Educational campaigns must actively challenge this notion, emphasizing that domestic violence is a serious crime that affects all segments of society, regardless of socioeconomic status, ethnicity, or educational background. This requires clear, consistent messaging disseminated through various channels, from public service announcements and social media campaigns to school curricula and community workshops.

School curricula should incorporate age-appropriate lessons on healthy relationships, consent, and recognizing the signs of abuse. These lessons must move beyond simple definitions; they should provide students with practical skills to identify unhealthy relationship dynamics, understand the cycle of violence, and develop strategies for seeking help for themselves or others. Role-playing scenarios, interactive discussions, and access to trusted adult mentors can reinforce these lessons and create a safe space for open dialogue. The goal is not to instill fear but to empower young people with the knowledge and confidence to navigate relationships safely and responsibly.

Furthermore, educational initiatives must reach beyond schools and engage families directly. Parents often struggle to recognize or address abusive behavior within their own families, partly due to cultural norms, fear of family disruption, or a lack of understanding. Family-centered workshops and support groups can provide a crucial platform for learning about domestic violence, understanding the dynamics of abusive relationships, and developing coping strategies. These programs should incorporate sensitivity to diverse family structures and cultural contexts, ensuring that the information resonates with and is accessible to a wide range of participants. Peer-to-peer support within these groups can be invaluable, fostering a sense of community and shared experience.

Community-wide initiatives play a crucial role in fostering a culture of awareness and prevention. Community events, public forums, and partnerships with local organizations can raise awareness and provide access to critical resources. These events should not simply deliver information but create opportunities for meaningful dialogue and engagement. By bringing together community leaders, law enforcement professionals, victim advocates, and community members, these forums can establish vital networks of support and create a stronger collective response to domestic violence.

In addition to awareness campaigns, effective community strategies must focus on building supportive networks and increasing access to resources. This includes providing readily available information about local shelters, hotlines, legal aid services, and mental health support. Collaborations with local businesses, faith-based organizations, and community centers can ensure that this information is widely accessible and easily disseminated. The aim is to remove barriers to seeking help, enabling victims to access the support they need when they need it most. These resources must be culturally sensitive and linguistically accessible, ensuring that all members of the community have equal access to critical services.

Empowerment is inextricably linked to education. Simply raising awareness is insufficient; communities must be equipped with the tools and resources to act effectively. This involves training community members to become active bystanders, intervening safely and appropriately when witnessing potentially abusive situations. Bystander intervention training programs teach individuals how to recognize the signs of abuse, intervene safely, and support victims. These programs can help to shift the cultural norm that allows abuse to go unchecked, empowering individuals to take action and create a safer environment for everyone.

Furthermore, the role of media literacy cannot be overstated. In the digital age, social media and online platforms play a significant role in shaping perceptions and influencing behavior. Educational programs must focus on responsible media consumption, teaching individuals how to critically evaluate information related to relationships and domestic violence, and avoid perpetuating harmful stereotypes or myths. This also includes addressing the issue of online harassment and cyberstalking, which have become increasingly prevalent forms of abuse. Developing media literacy skills empowers individuals to navigate the digital landscape safely and critically assess the information they encounter.

The legal system also plays a critical role in empowering communities. Accessible legal aid services are essential for victims to pursue justice and secure protective measures. Furthermore, the legal system must adapt to the changing nature of domestic violence, including the increased use of technology in abusive relationships. Legal professionals need training in digital forensics and the intricacies of online abuse to effectively represent victims and ensure perpetrators are held accountable for their actions. This includes awareness of coercive control tactics, often more subtle than physical violence, and how they manifest in digital interactions.

Finally, long-term success relies on ongoing evaluation and data collection. Monitoring the effectiveness of educational programs and community initiatives allows for adjustments and improvements based on real-world feedback. This ongoing process of evaluation ensures that programs are continually adapted to meet the evolving needs of the community and address emerging challenges. By creating a system of continuous improvement, communities can build more resilient responses and create a lasting impact in the fight against domestic violence. The legacy of Gabby Petito demands not just systemic reforms within law enforcement, but also a fundamental cultural shift that prioritizes prevention, empowerment, and support for victims. Only through a comprehensive, community-based approach can we truly hope to prevent future tragedies and build a society free from the scourge of domestic violence.

Moving Forward Continuing the Conversation

The outpouring of grief and outrage following Gabby Petito's death reverberated far beyond the immediate circle of her family and friends. It ignited a national conversation about domestic violence, a conversation that, while long overdue, had previously lacked the sustained intensity and public attention this case garnered. The ubiquitous nature of social media, ironically the same platform that showcased Gabby's seemingly idyllic life, played a crucial role in amplifying the story, disseminating information at an unprecedented speed and bringing the tragedy into millions of homes. This unprecedented level of public engagement, however, brought with it both opportunities and challenges.

The intense media scrutiny, while raising awareness of domestic violence, also risked sensationalizing the tragedy, potentially overshadowing the systemic issues at play. The focus on Gabby's story, while undeniably heartbreaking, also risked creating a narrative that prioritized individual cases over the broader societal problem. The danger lies in becoming so captivated by the drama of a single tragedy that we overlook the larger patterns of abuse and violence playing out every day in countless other relationships. The challenge was—and remains—to channel this intense public interest into meaningful, sustainable action.

Moving forward requires a sustained commitment to several key areas. Firstly, the legal system must continue to adapt and improve its response to domestic violence. While significant progress has been made in recognizing coercive control as a form of abuse, further efforts are needed to ensure that laws accurately reflect the complexities of modern relationships, particularly those played out within the digital sphere. This means providing law enforcement officers with adequate training in identifying and addressing the subtle signs of manipulation and control, often manifested through seemingly innocuous digital interactions—tracking apps, controlling access to social media, or even the constant barrage of emotionally manipulative messages.

Furthermore, access to justice for victims must be improved. This includes ensuring that victims have access to legal representation, regardless of their financial circumstances. Legal aid services play a crucial role in ensuring that victims are not left to navigate the legal system alone, often facing intimidation and pressure from abusers and their families. Moreover, the availability of protective orders and restraining orders must be streamlined and made readily accessible to those in need. The goal is not simply to prosecute perpetrators but to provide comprehensive support to victims so they can escape abusive situations safely and rebuild their lives.

Beyond the legal system, significant improvements are required in the provision of support services for victims of domestic violence. This encompasses a broad range of resources, including shelters, hotlines, counseling, and financial assistance. Access to these services must be readily available, culturally appropriate, and free from barriers that can prevent victims from seeking help. Language accessibility, culturally sensitive outreach programs, and the provision of support services for diverse communities are all critical components of a successful response. Moreover, these services must acknowledge and address the complex interplay of factors that contribute to domestic violence, including mental health issues, substance abuse, and economic hardship.

Public awareness campaigns need to evolve beyond simply raising awareness and must actively challenge harmful social norms that perpetuate domestic violence. These campaigns should move beyond simply highlighting the statistics and individual tragedies and focus on shifting cultural attitudes that normalize or excuse abusive behavior. By promoting healthy relationship skills, teaching individuals how to recognize the signs of abuse, and encouraging bystander intervention, we can create a societal shift toward a culture of prevention. The focus must be on empowering individuals to recognize unhealthy relationship dynamics, encouraging them to seek help for themselves or intervene safely when witnessing potentially abusive situations.

The role of social media in disseminating information about domestic violence is a double-edged sword. While it has the potential to raise awareness and facilitate support networks, it also carries the risk of spreading misinformation, perpetuating harmful stereotypes, and fueling online harassment. Media literacy education becomes crucial in helping individuals navigate this complex digital landscape, equipping them with the skills to critically evaluate information and engage responsibly online. This means promoting critical thinking skills, teaching individuals how to recognize biased reporting or manipulative online content, and highlighting the potential for online harassment to escalate into real-world violence.

The ongoing conversation surrounding Gabby Petito's death highlights the enduring nature of systemic issues related to domestic violence. It's not enough to simply react to individual tragedies; we must build systems and structures that actively prevent violence before it occurs. This requires a multi-faceted approach, incorporating educational initiatives in schools and communities, effective law enforcement training, readily accessible support services for survivors, and an ongoing commitment to challenging societal norms that perpetuate abusive behavior.

The legacy of Gabby Petito's tragic death should not be solely defined by the horrific circumstances surrounding her demise, but rather by the lasting impact it had on fostering a more proactive and comprehensive approach to domestic violence prevention. This demands a collective responsibility: a commitment from individuals, communities, and governing bodies to create a society where such tragedies become increasingly rare. The challenge remains in translating the initial surge of public attention into sustained, long-term action, ensuring that the conversation continues, evolving and adapting to meet the dynamic challenges presented by this ever-evolving issue. The call for change should not wane; rather, it should strengthen, fueled by a commitment to protecting victims and holding perpetrators accountable. Only through persistent effort and a renewed dedication to this vital cause can we hope to prevent future tragedies and create a more equitable and safer world for all. The fight against domestic violence is a marathon, not a sprint, and the momentum generated by Gabby Petito's case must be harnessed and channeled to achieve lasting change. The details of her story may fade from headlines, but the need for ongoing dialogue, action, and unwavering support for survivors must not.